Uncoverings 2000

Uncoverings 2000

Volume 21 of the Research Papers
of the American Quilt Study Group

Edited by Virginia Gunn

Copyright © 2000 by the
American Quilt Study Group
All Rights Reserved

Copyright note: This is a collective work. AQSG holds the copyright to this volume and any reproduction of it in whole. Right to individual articles are held by the authors. Requests for permission to quote or reproduce material from any article should be addressed to the author.

Published by the American Quilt Study Group
35th and Holdredge Street
Lincoln, Nebraska 68504-0737

Manufactured in the United States.

Uncoverings is indexed in:
America: History and Life
ARTbibliographies
BHA (Bibliography of the History of Art)
Clothing and Textile Arts Index
Feminist Periodicals
Historical Abstracts
MLA International Bibliography
Sociological Abstracts

ISBN 1-877859-16-8   ISSN 0277-0628
Library of Congress catalog number: 81-649486

Cover: Silk Cigar Ribbon Table Cover, maker unknown
Collection of Ethel Ewert Abrahams
Photograph courtesy of Kauffman Museum,
Bethel College, North Newton, Kansas.

Contents

Preface   vii

RESEARCH PAPERS

An "Old-Fashioned Quilting" in 1910
    Laurel Horton   1

Textiles and Cooperative Commerce in Colonial America: The Example of William McCormick
    Xenia E. Cord   27

Creating a New Tradition: Quilting in Tonga
    Phyllis S. Herda   57

"Better Choose Me": Addictions to Tobacco, Collecting, and Quilting, 1880-1920
    Ethel Ewert Abrahams and
    Rachel K. Pannabecker   79

Hubert Ver Mehren and Home Art Studios
    Susan Price Miller   107

"Petting the Fabric": Medium and the Creative Process
    Lisa Gabbert   137

1999 SEMINAR KEYNOTE ADDRESS

Quilts and Their Stories:
Revealing a Hidden History
    Marsha MacDowell   155

Authors and Editor   167

Index   171

Preface

American Quilt Study Group members will gather on the University of Nebraska-Lincoln campus from October 13-15, 2000 to attend the organization's twenty-first annual seminar. Michael James, renowned art quiltmaker and now instructor in the university's College of Human Resources and Family Sciences, will deliver the keynote address "In the Beginning: Musings on the Birth of the Studio Art Quilt Movement."

Members will attend a dedication ceremony to celebrate the new location of the AQSG Research Library Collection, started by founder Sally Garoutte and augmented by members and friends for the past twenty years. Recognition will also be given to other charter members of AQSG.

A look back at twenty years of research accomplishments reveals that the studies contributed to the various volumes of *Uncoverings* have indeed proven to be seminal works undergirding quilt research. A look through the notes and bibliographies of most significant works related to quilt history demonstrate that articles first published in *Uncoverings* have provided the foundation for continuing research and interpretation. The authors contributing to this volume share important work that will add to the depth and breadth of quilt study as AQSG begins its third decade of work.

In the first two articles the authors demonstrate how careful analysis of verbal documents offers new insights about periods that have received little attention. Laurel Horton unraveled the complex context of a local quilting event that took place in Seneca, South Carolina, in 1910. Following the clues offered in a brief newspaper report she focuses attention on how women used quilts and quiltmaking in casual ways to achieve personal and social goals.

Xenia Cord used information from an unpublished handwritten eighteenth-century account book to reconstruct the fascinating story of William McCormick, a linen weaver from Virginia who worked in southwestern Pennsylvania during the Revolutionary War era. She discusses and interprets the importance of textiles and cooperative commerce on the early western frontier.

Phyllis Herda's extensive fieldwork in the islands of Tonga provides information that adds to our knowledge of quiltmaking's international aspects. She documents the ways Tongan women have expanded their traditional textile production to include quiltmaking. The study highlights Tongan quilts and their association with important life-cycle rituals from birth to death.

Lisa Gabbert used field study and folklore techniques to explore the relationships between artists and their chosen medium. Her study of a group of central Idaho quilters revealed the central, but underacknowledged, role that the sensory aspects of fabric play in the fiber arts process. Her work suggests that the feel of the fabric provides an essential dynamic in quiltmaking.

Susan Price Miller makes an important contribution to our knowledge of twentieth-century quilt pattern designers with her careful study of Hubert Ver Mehren of Des Moines, Iowa. Her research gives long-overdue attention to the artist, entrepreneur, and marketing expert behind the well-known Home Art Studios business that provided quilt patterns and pieced quilt designs in the 1920s and 1930s.

Ethel Ewert Abrahams and Rachel Pannabecker collaborated to interpret quilts made from cigar ribbons, cigarette silks, and tobacco flannels during the late-nineteenth and early-twentieth centuries. Their study shows how turn-of-the-century quiltmakers creatively responded to the novel and aggressive marketing techniques used by the tobacco companies. An example of this interesting genre of quilts graces the cover of this volume.

The book ends with the keynote address that Marsha MacDowell, a recognized expert in folk art and then president of AQSG, delivered at the 1999 annual seminar held in East Lansing, Michigan. This thought-provoking speech called attention to the importance of oral

Preface

histories as sources of information and to the challenges oral accounts often pose for researchers.

Quilts continue to provide a wonderful window to understanding culture. They touch the lives of the folk as well as the elite, of men as well as women, and of diverse ages, backgrounds, and circumstances both in America and around the world. Quilt history is definitely alive and well.

An "Old-Fashioned Quilting" in 1910

Laurel Horton

A newspaper report of a local quilting event in Seneca, South Carolina, in 1910, recorded the participation of a group of eight women. The event is examined within the context of other local social events and quilting activities in an attempt to determine the significance of this event for its participants. The event narrative reveals the existence of a practical joke performed by the hostess as part of her enactment of an "old-fashioned quilting." An unintended response to the event illustrates some of the tensions created by competing values among different social classes and by the changing roles of women. This study demonstrates the complex context of a single quilting event and focuses attention on women who were not active quiltmakers but who used quilts and quiltmaking to achieve personal and social goals.

> On last Tuesday, Mrs. J. H. Thompson entertained her friends at an old-fashioned quilting, which proved a happy climax to the many delightful social affairs of the holidays.[1]

This opening statement prefaced a detailed item in the "Local Matters About Seneca" column of the January 12, 1910, issue of the *Keowee Courier*, a weekly newspaper published in Walhalla, South Carolina, the county seat of Oconee County (see figure 1).[2] This paper is the result of additional research conducted in an attempt to determine the *significance* of this event to the participants in this particular time and place. There is no evidence that suggests that these women met to quilt on a regular basis. Instead, this appears to have been a one-time event presented by the hostess as a novel form of entertainment within the local social structure.

Uncoverings 2000

The Setting

Located in the northwestern corner of the state, Oconee County adjoins Georgia and North Carolina. The county's boundary encompasses forests, rivers, and rolling farmland in the foothills of the Blue Ridge mountains. By 1910, there were several recently constructed textile mills in the county, but the principal economic activities continued to be agriculture and forestry. According to the 1910 census, Oconee County had a predominantly rural population of 27,337. That year the town of Walhalla, established in 1849, had a population of 1,595, while that of the town of Seneca, founded in 1872, had grown to 1,313.[3]

During the early twentieth century, the *Keowee Courier* published a mix of local, state, national, and international news items; some syndicated features; local and national advertisements; railroad schedules; and commentary. Typical of rural newspapers serving predominantly rural areas, a major feature of the *Courier* was the community news columns submitted by local correspondents scattered throughout the county. To a modern eye, community news columns include items that seem trivial, meaningless, or even comical, such as "Miss Sue Haley spent the week-end with Miss Sue Daly," or "W. H. Hughes has recovered from a severe attack of erysipelas [a skin inflammation], and his friends are delighted to see him out again." But for a predominantly rural population without telephones, connected by unpaved roads over hilly terrain, the publication of such news served a vital communicative function.

Women's Social Events

The newspaper account of Mrs. Thompson's quilting was only one of a large number of items listed in the community news columns. While individual correspondents included short accounts of visits and illnesses, by far the most extensive coverage was given to descriptions of social events, especially daytime women's gatherings. During the late-nineteenth and early-twentieth centuries, women's voluntary associations proliferated throughout the country. Women formed clubs

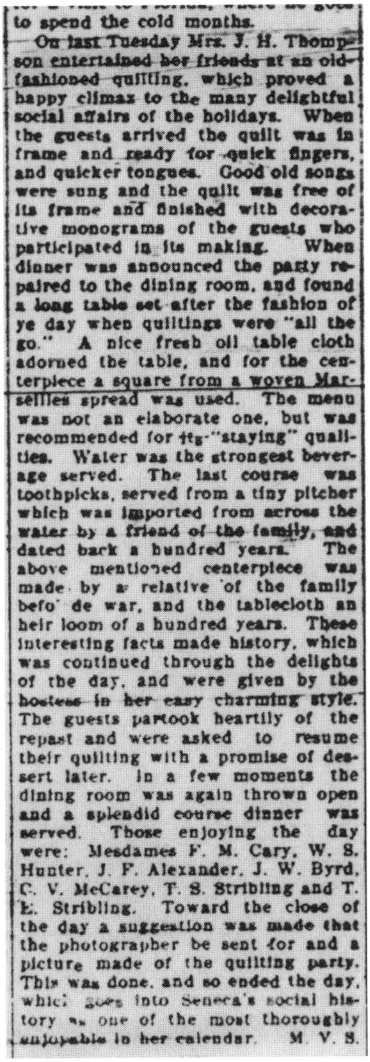

to spend the cold months.

On last Tuesday Mrs. J. H. Thompson entertained her friends at an old-fashioned quilting, which proved a happy climax to the many delightful social affairs of the holidays. When the guests arrived the quilt was in frame and ready for quick fingers, and quicker tongues. Good old songs were sung and the quilt was free of its frame and finished with decorative monograms of the guests who participated in its making. When dinner was announced the party repaired to the dining room, and found a long table set after the fashion of ye day when quiltings were "all the go." A nice fresh oil table cloth adorned the table, and for the centerpiece a square from a woven Marseilles spread was used. The menu was not an elaborate one, but was recommended for its "staying" qualities. Water was the strongest beverage served. The last course was toothpicks, served from a tiny pitcher which was imported from across the water by a friend of the family, and dated back a hundred years. The above mentioned centerpiece was made by a relative of the family befo' de war, and the tablecloth an heir loom of a hundred years. These interesting facts made history, which was continued through the delights of the day, and were given by the hostess in her easy charming style. The guests partook heartily of the repast and were asked to resume their quilting with a promise of dessert later. In a few moments the dining room was again thrown open and a splendid course dinner was served. Those enjoying the day were: Mesdames F. M. Cary, W. S. Hunter, J. F. Alexander, J. W. Byrd, C. V. McCarey, T. S. Stribling and T. E. Stribling. Toward the close of the day a suggestion was made that the photographer be sent for and a picture made of the quilting party. This was done, and so ended the day, which goes into Seneca's social history as one of the most thoroughly enjoyable in her calendar. M. V. S.

Figure 1: The published report of Mrs. Thompson's "old-fashioned quilting" appeared in the January 12, 1910, issue of the *Keowee Courier*.

and societies for a variety of purposes, including religious and missionary work, literary and art study, and civic improvement.[4] Those that have received the least attention from historians are those formed primarily for social purposes.

The women who joined local clubs "were drawn for the most part from a small minority of the prosperous, usually wives and daughters of substantial farmers, or of white-collar and professional men. Thanks to the increasing availability of factory-made goods and of poorly paid black and white household servants, these women were relieved of much domestic responsibility."[5] The pages of the *Keowee Courier* document the social interactions of the wives of farmers and merchants through narratives of club meeting activities.

Newspaper Reports of Quilting Activity

Although for the period 1909-1910 there are relatively few specific mentions of quiltmaking activity in the *Keowee Courier*, the meetings of local women's groups typically included an hour of "fancywork," usually defined as decorative or ornamental needlework, such as crochet, knitting, or embroidery.[6] For example, the newspaper reported a weekly meeting of the Emery Club of Walhalla: "For an hour or more fancy work furnished occupation for the busy fingers, while the latest news, fashion dots, etc., gave play to the busy brains."[7] The inclusion of such domestic activity in a social context may have helped dispel criticism that the meetings were distracting women from their responsibilities to homes and families.[8]

Of the newspaper items that mentioned quiltmaking activity, the majority involved church groups and Sunshine workers making quilts for charity. [9] All three references during 1909, and nine of twelve references for 1910, described charity quiltings in the outlying rural communities of Fair Play, Coneross, and Bountyland, not in the towns of Seneca or Walhalla. The products of these quiltings were designated for the Connie Maxwell, Epworth, and Thornwell Orphanages, all in South Carolina, and the "Blind Babies' home in New York."[10] Although the reports of charity quiltings, particularly those held in the homes of individuals, occasionally included descriptions of refreshments and comments that the participants enjoyed themselves, these reports typically placed more emphasis on the number of quilts completed and their intended disposition than on the social amenities of the event.[11] In contrast, the account of Mrs. Thompson's quilting dwelt on the social nature of the occasion.

Old-Fashioned Quilting

Entertaining the Ladies

> *When the guests arrived the quilt was in frame and ready for quick fingers, and quicker tongues. Good old songs were sung and the quilt was free of its frame and finished with decorative monograms of the guests who participated in its making.*

A reading of hundreds of published accounts of ladies' social events of this era reveals that the principal goal to which hostesses aspired was to provide novel entertainment within an atmosphere of refinement and gentility. Katherine C. Grier described "gentility" in this context as an "eighteenth-century European cultural ideal, . . . a model of personal excellence originating in the uppermost classes of society, [which] stressed individual cultivation and social display."[12] The chief elements of a successful social event were elaborate decorations, sumptuous refreshment, and delightful entertainment, and the hostess who could provide these with little apparent effort received special commendations from the newspaper correspondent. The Seneca correspondent to the *Keowee Courier* submitted this detailed account of one event:

> Miss Mary Cherry was hostess to the Gossipers last week at a "St. Patrick's Day" entertainment. Elaborate preparations were shown in the decorations and in the refreshments, both of which were in keeping with the spirit of the occasion. Progressive hearts was played, the score cards representing the shamrock. For the highest score, Miss Sue Thompson was awarded the prize, a hat pin set with an emerald. At the close of the game the guests were ushered into the dining room where a three-course luncheon was served. The guests were seated about the large dining table, which was ablaze with many tapers of green candelabra. The centerpiece was a mirror decoration representing, of course, the Emerald Isle, native moss and ferns being used in its perfect representation. Bonbon dishes of mints in green were seen on the table. Ferns and palms were used in pyramidal shape, the beauty of which was greatly enhanced by the use of lighted candles, and tracings of ivy were seen on the curtains. Favors of gauze shamrock were found at the places, which were designated by hand-painted place cards. The pièce de résistance was the elegant cake, which was embossed in most artistic design, showing the dainty shamrock and miniature pipes. There was a full attendance of the members who voted it one of the most thoroughly delightful meetings in the history of the Gossipers.[13]

Uncoverings 2000

Mrs. Thompson's "old-fashioned quilting" must be examined in the context of other weekly, daytime, women's social events of this time and place. Although the guests were invited to sit at a quilt frame and stitch, the quilt itself, the quilting activity, and the "good old songs" functioned as props for the novel entertainment provided by the hostess. The designation "old-fashioned" suggests that the activity was perceived as more typical of the past than the present.[14] No detail is provided in the newspaper account of the physical description or the intended disposition of the resulting quilt. Mrs. Thompson's quilt was "finished with decorative monograms of the guests," which suggests that she intended to keep it as a memento of the occasion rather than to donate it to charity.

An Elaborate Joke

The published narrative of this event described an elaborate practical joke designed by the hostess. After working on the quilt during the morning, the guests anticipated being served a lavish luncheon. But the hostess continued her interpretation of the "old-fashioned" theme through her choice of luncheon decorations and menu.

> *When dinner was announced the party repaired to the dining room, and found a long table set after the fashion of ye day when quiltings were "all the go." A nice fresh oil table cloth adorned the table, and for the centerpiece a square from a woven Marseilles spread was used. The menu was not an elaborate one, but was recommended for its "staying" qualities. Water was the strongest beverage served.*

The correspondent relied on understated humor to convey to her readers that the spread provided by the hostess was meager. Traditional rules governing hospitality in Western culture require that hosts provide ample refreshment for invited guests, and at the same time preclude guests from commenting on any deficiencies. Although Mrs. Thompson committed an offense by not providing the expected elaborate repast for her friends, the guests would not risk further offense by mentioning the deficiency. Likewise, the correspondent, herself one of the guests, could not describe the spartan nature of the offering in her narrative directly and instead relied on subtle irony. Her narrative provided subtle clues to the bogus nature of the meal. Describing the menu as "not an elaborate one" would have tipped off contemporary readers immediately, because a universal paradigm for such events is a meal that is "sumptuous," "delightful," or at the very least, "tempting." The further comment, "Recommended for its 'staying' qualities," contrasts with the usual epithet in such cases, "dainty." Providing water rather than, perhaps, tea or punch also suggests that the spread was not up to expectations.

> *The last course was toothpicks, served from a tiny pitcher which was imported from across the water by a friend of the family, and dated back a hundred years. The above mentioned centerpiece was made by a relative of the family befo' de war, and the tablecloth an heir loom of a hundred years. These interesting facts made history, which was continued through the delights of the day and were given by the hostess in her easy, charming style.*

Describing toothpicks as "the last course," suggesting their use in public, would have struck contemporary readers as uncouth, further marking this event as an anomaly. In addition to conveying the humor of the situation, however, the correspondent also reported the significance of certain material objects used by the hostess to enhance her "old-fashioned" theme. The description of the hostess's "easy, charming style" may suggest the correspondent's admiration for her ability to maintain the hoax.

> *The guests partook heartily of the repast and were asked to resume their quilting with a promise of dessert later. In a few moments the dining room was again thrown open and a splendid course dinner was served.*

Although the guests may have "partaken heartily" of the first meal, they clearly could not have sated their appetites. They were ushered from the dining room, still uncertain of the hostess's motives. It would have been only after the dining room was reopened to reveal the actual meal that the elaborate joke could be acknowledged, allowing the guests and their hostess to share the laughter along with the "splendid course dinner."

Uncoverings 2000

Mrs. Thompson's Guests

> *Those enjoying the day were: Mesdames F. M. Cary, W. S. Hunter, J. F. Alexander, J. W. Byrd, C. V. McCarey, T. S. Stribling, and T. E. Stribling. Toward the close of the day a suggestion was made that the photographer be sent for and a picture made of the quilting party. This was done, and so ended the day, which goes into Seneca's social history as one of the most thoroughly enjoyable in her calendar. M. V. S.*

A photograph of the eight women who attended the quilting is published in a book compiled by Frances Holleman (see figure 2).[15] The portrait does not include a quilt, but it may well be the photograph mentioned in the narrative. Details of the clothing suggest that the photograph dates from 1909 or 1910.[16] The published photograph is credited to Miss Nora Carver, who with her sister Cora "operated a studio on North Depot Street and later upstairs in the Harper Building across from the park."[17] Either studio location would have been an easy walk from Mrs. Thompson's home, and there is no record of another photographer in business in Seneca during 1910.

The notation that a photograph was taken to document a social event is unique among the hundreds of published narratives in this newspaper. It seems to be an indication of a feeling of communality and cohesiveness. The participants wanted their participation in the event to be recorded. From additional issues of the *Keowee Courier*, census data, church histories, cemetery records, and books on local history, it is possible to piece together admittedly incomplete portraits of the eight participants in Mrs. Thompson's quilting.

The hostess, Lida Alexander Thompson (1869-1941), was the daughter of Henry F. Alexander, a Confederate veteran, and Rebecca Doyle Alexander. The Alexanders first lived in Walhalla, and in the 1890s they moved to Seneca, where Lida's father was engaged in the real estate business and served for a time as Treasurer of Oconee County. In 1891, Lida married James H. Thompson, the son of Seneca's first mayor. The couple had one son, Alfred H., born in 1893. Lida (also listed variously as Lidie, Alida, or Lyda) Thompson was thirty-nine years old in 1910.[18]

Annie Mildred Fant Cary (1866-1941) was a native of Anderson, a

Old-Fashioned Quilting

Figure 2: The eight women who participated in Mrs. Thompson's "old-fashioned quilting" were identified by the author of a local history publication. Photograph from Frances Holleman, *The City of Seneca, South Carolina, The City of Opportunity: Its Centennial, 1873–1973*.

town thirty miles southeast of Seneca. In 1888, she married Frank M. Cary (or Carey), who was self-employed as a cotton dealer, a director of the First Citizens Bank in Seneca, and served as a state representative. In 1910, the Carys lived with their six children, ranging in age from two to twenty. Also living in the household were Frank's twenty-two-year-old niece—a bookkeeper in a dry goods store—and Sallie Clark, a black cook. In 1910, Annie Fant Cary was forty-four years old.[19]

Nina Dickinson Lewis Hunter (1867-1943) married William Simpson Hunter in 1886. William Hunter was a store owner and one of the organizers of the Citizens Bank in 1904. In 1910, Nina Hunter, age forty-three, lived with her husband and three daughters in their own home on North First Street. (Unlike many homes of this vintage close to the business district, the Hunter house still stands and has been renovated for offices.) Their oldest daughter Carrie L., age twenty-two, lived at home and listed her occupation as music teacher.[20]

Emma Scott Alexander (1873-1952) married James Franklin Alex-

Uncoverings 2000

ander in 1902. James Alexander was a bookkeeper in a dry goods store, and later was in partnership with Joseph W. Byrd for a short time before joining the Seneca Bank. In 1910, Emma Alexander, age thirty-six, lived in a rented home with her husband and their three small children. James F. Alexander was the younger brother of Lida Alexander Thompson, so Emma Alexander was the sister-in-law of the hostess.[21]

Personne Magee (or McGee) Byrd (1868-1918) was the wife of Joseph Wilson Byrd, who was a partner in a dry goods store and who served, at various times, as a town warden, a commissioner for the Light and Water Plant, and Treasurer of the Chamber of Commerce. Married in 1888, "Sonnie" and Joseph Byrd were living in Seneca in 1910, with their two sons. Clara L. Hunt, a twenty-five-year-old public schoolteacher, boarded with the family.[22]

Clara Verner McCarey (1868-1952) was the widow of James F. McCarey (or McCary) who was appointed Seneca postmaster in 1895 and died in 1901, at age thirty-four. In 1910, Clara McCarey, age forty-four, was living with her two children, James F., Jr., seventeen, and Clara Verner, Jr., ten. The accepted convention for formal address for a widow was to use her own initials rather than those of her late husband.[23]

Maude Verner Stribling (1879-1918) married Thomas Sligh Stribling in 1899. T. S. Stribling worked as a salesman in a hardware store. In 1910, Maude, age thirty, and her husband lived with their four young children. Their oldest daughter Mary Ida, or "Poppy," was later described as "a dedicated member" of the local D.A.R. chapter.[24]

Martha "Mattie" Verner Stribling (1861-1945) married Thomas Edward Stribling in 1889. Maude Verner, Clara Verner, and Mattie Verner were apparently not sisters, but they were no doubt part of the large and influential Verner family of Oconee County. Thomas S. Stribling and Thomas E. Stribling were second cousins. In 1910, Thomas E. Stribling owned a grocery store. In 1910, Mattie, age forty-seven, lived with her husband and their four children ranging in age from twelve to nineteen.[25] Mattie Verner Stribling served as the Seneca correspondent for the *Keowee Courier* for a number of years and is "M. V. S.," the author of the narrative of Mrs. Thompson's quilting and other local Seneca items.

Of these eight women, six were in their forties. The two younger women were Maude Verner Stribling, twenty-nine, and Emma Scott Alexander, thirty-six. The eight women had a total of twenty-six living children, whose ages in 1910 ranged from two to twenty-two, and at least two more who had died. Although at least one, Sonnie Byrd, had taught school before her marriage, none of the women were employed outside the home.

One of the eight employed a live-in cook; the others almost certainly employed daily service workers. The intersection of North First and Oak streets, near which all the women lived, is only three blocks from the location, then and now, of the African-American neighborhood in which the Seneca Institute for Negroes was established in 1899. As this was the only school of its type in the area, many black families moved into Seneca so that their children could attend the Institute. Graduates of the school recalled that their parents did laundry and other work for white families living nearby. While nationally the twentieth century saw a decline in the employment of household service workers, Mattie Stribling noted in her column, "The servant question is not the problem with Seneca housewives that it once was. . . . It is a fact that the supply exceeds the demand in Seneca."[26] These women were in good position, financially and logistically, to employ household or child-care workers.

All eight of the women had connections with the Seneca Presbyterian Church. Annie Fant Cary did not join the Church, though her husband had served as a deacon and as secretary/treasurer of the Sunday School. Lida Thompson and her parents were members of the Church, but her husband and son were not. Maude and Mattie Stribling, along with their children, were members, but not their husbands. The other four women, their husbands, and their children were all members. Sonnie Byrd taught Sunday School, and Mattie Stribling served on the music committee and took part in regional church meetings to merge the Ladies Aid and the Missionary Society. Clara McCarey presented the Church with a mahogany table in memory of her late husband, while Nina Hunter later donated a stained glass window in honor of her husband, who died in 1918. Unlike established rural churches of this era, the Seneca Presbyterian Church did not own land for a cem-

Uncoverings 2000

etery. All eight of the women, their husbands, and many of their children are buried in the nondenominational Mountain View Cemetery, a few blocks north of their homes in Seneca.[27]

The husbands of all eight women were engaged in local commercial ventures. The men were successful merchants, cotton brokers, and bankers, and they took an active part in local government. Established in 1872, Seneca was one of the numerous small towns spawned by new railroad connections built during the Reconstruction period following the Civil War. The town's population had expanded rapidly from 382 in 1880, to 1,313 in 1910. Seneca's commercial district grew in response to increased demand for goods and services.[28]

As a new town, Seneca society was a mixture of the descendants of old, respected early Oconee County families, such as the Alexanders, Doyles, Striblings, and Verners, and more recent arrivals attracted by business prospects. It is not clear how much rivalry or snobbery there might have been between the commercially based Seneca residents and the older agriculturally based families in Walhalla and surrounding rural communities. Certainly, some of Seneca's business leaders—and their wives—were from older families.

Local Women's Clubs

Additional research turned up evidence of the participation of these eight women in local organizations. In 1896, twelve Seneca women met to form the Once-A-Week Club, "in order to furnish a stimulus for the study of general literature and for the purpose of social enjoyment and mutual improvement." This club is significant because two years later its members hosted the state-wide organizational meeting that resulted in the formation of the South Carolina Federation of Women's Clubs. The Once-A-Week Club also headed an effort to establish a local library in 1896, and supported activities to improve local schools.[29]

Members of the Once-A-Week Club included Mesdames Byrd, Cary, Hunter, McCarey, and T. E. Stribling. Between 1898 and 1901, however, all five of these women had either resigned from the Club or ceased attending meetings, although there is no indication of the reasons for their departures.[30]

Old-Fashioned Quilting

The Blossom Girls

According to Holleman in information accompanying the photograph, however, these eight women had formed their own club, the Blossom Girls, a group "interested in self-expression through projects which they promoted. To finance these projects they presented plays in the local Opera House, which was located in the Citizens Bank Building. The name of the club was derived from the title of one of their early productions."[31]

Additional research, however, offers a somewhat different account. The names of these eight women appear frequently in social pages in the *Keowee Courier* in various combinations and along with the names of other women. On February 17, 1909, following the account of an elaborate Valentine party hosted for the Once-A-Week Club, there appears the announcement of the formation of a new group:

> Another organization which promises to be replete with genuine pleasure is the Every Tuesday Social Circle, which was organized last week at the home of Mrs. C. V. McCarey. The object is purely social, as the name indicates, and will meet every Tuesday, as is also indicated by the name. There is [sic] no officers, and Shattuck's manual is an unknown quantity with them. We are told that the deliberations are sub rosa—so much in refutation of the impression afloat that it is to be in effect the 'Senior Gossipers.'"[32]

The list of attendees includes five of the women in question, along with two additional names. At the second meeting, Mrs. J. W. Byrd joined the group. Only the two younger women were not listed as members. (Carrie Hunter, the twenty-one-year-old daughter of Mrs. W. S. Hunter, was a member of the Gossipers, a group of young unmarried women.) There is further evidence that the "Blossom Girls" were not actually a club but an outgrowth of a church fundraising event. Mattie Stribling reported in her column in October 1909:

> Yesterday afternoon the Ladies' Aid Society of the Presbyterian church met with Mrs. W. S. Hunter. It was a full meeting, and the members were in a working mood, judging by the following account of the business attended to: It was decided that the society support an orphan at the Thornwell Orphanage; that the society start a church fund, for the purpose of assisting

13

in building a new church; that the 'Blossom Show' be repeated during the Christmas holidays. This play will be remembered by many of our citizens, and on account of its popularity the members of the society have decided to accede to repeated requests to repeat it.[33]

In November, Mattie Stribling provided an update on the progress of the entertainment:

We called attention two weeks ago to the fact that the Ladies' Aid Society of the Presbyterian church would repeat the Blossom Show in the near future. The time has been set for the first week in December. It will be seen that new talent has been added, and there are also many new and attractive features. The show was recognized as being one of the best ever given here, and repeated and continuous requests for its repetition induced the society to comply, and it is useless to say that with superior local talent the show will be a marked improvement over the first presentation.[34]

Six of the women in question were named as participating in this performance, along with Nina Hunter's musical daughter and Sonnie Byrd's boarding schoolteacher. Neither Emma Alexander nor Clara Verner McCarey was listed in the cast, although the latter was described in the same week's column as "suffering an attack of grippe [influenza]" and might have been indisposed.[35] A week before the performance, Mattie Stribling presented this enticement:

The "Musical Bouquet," or, more familiarly speaking, the "Blossom Show," will be presented in the opera house Tuesday evening, December 7th by local talent. Great pains have been taken to make the show a success, and it goes without saying that it will be the best amateur performance ever given in Seneca. The cast is a full one and composed of our best talent. Mrs. J. W. Byrd, as Ma Blossom, is exactly what would be expected from her by those who know her capabilities in this line, and Mrs. W. S. Hunter, as Grandma, exceeds the expectations of the most sanguine, the role being a decided departure from anything done by her hitherto. The gals, seven in number, including the twins, the "bashful gals," etc., are all good, and a rare treat is in store for the public.[36]

The Citizens Bank building was constructed in 1905, on the corner of Main and Fair Play streets. According to Holleman, "On the second floor was a spacious hall known, first, as The Opera House; later, as a Social Hall, where the dances were held." W. S. Hunter and F. M. Cary

Old-Fashioned Quilting

were among the first directors of the Citizens Bank. Thus the Blossom Girls had access to the use of the second floor hall through the involvement in the Citizens Bank of two of their spouses.[37] Following the December 7th performance, Mattie Stribling offered this review:

> The appearance of the "Blossom Family" at the opera house last Tuesday night has been the talk of the town ever since, and it is not putting it extravagantly to say it was a "howling success." Everything contributed to make it a success—the audience, which was large and representative, the weather which was fair after a big rain—and the sympathy of the audience was assured immediately as the curtain rose. One round of applause followed another, and it is not exaggerating the truth to say that it was the biggest hit ever seen here. Our readers are familiar with the cast, and all the parts were splendidly sustained. As has been frequently said, every part was exactly suited to the cast, and a number of our best citizens have expressed a wish that it be repeated. One of our public officials said he would give a dollar to see Miss Doolittle again, the character so admirably interpreted by Mrs. F. M. Cary. Mrs. W. S. Hunter, as Grandma, was "real acting," and her most intimate friends did not recognize her, so perfect was her make-up. Mrs. J. W. Byrd, as Ma Blossom, fully met the expectations of her friends and sustained her reputation as leading lady. Miss Doolittle, who is visiting her sister, Mrs. Hardscratch, in the neighborhood, calls to 'get one of the gals to take her picture,' which she desires for her beau, Elder Snifkin. Her make-up, and the poses she effects while sitting for the picture are something indescribable. Grandma begs Miss Doolittle to 'set a spell,' and they discuss the love affairs of herself and the elder. The local hits were fierce, and were given in inimitable style by Mrs. J. H. Thompson, who also, with Miss Maud Hopkins, represents the timid gals. Space forbids our giving further details of the play, but suffice it to say that should the company be induced to appear again, a packed house will greet them, and standing room will go at a premium.[38]

The Blossom Show was indeed repeated on December 31 with, according to Stribling, "a new music program and new local hits. It may be well to add here that those who suffered from local hits before may be comforted with the fact that they will not be hit again." There were changes in the cast, including the addition of Clara Verner McCarey as "one of the twins." Stribling's report indicates "There have been several inquiries from neighboring towns, . . . which shows how the reputation of the Blossom family as entertainers has spread abroad."[39]

Following the second performance, a review appeared in the Sen-

Uncoverings 2000

eca weekly newspaper, *Farm and Factory*, which up to this point had not reported local social events to the extent of the Walhalla paper's coverage. The unidentified reporter described the second performance of the "famous play" in this way:

> The attendance was large, which showed the appreciation of the acting of the ladies forming the "Blossom Family." The music and singing were exceptionally good. There was several changes in the make-up of the play, but all the ladies were equal to the occasion. . . . Quite a neat sum was realized from the door receipts.[40]

This reporter confirmed Mattie Stribling's report of the success of the event, including a report of the financial rewards that Stribling had not mentioned.

The glowing report in *Farm and Factory* contrasts with that of Mattie Stribling, who briefly noted that "a splendid house greeted the Blossom Family last Friday night." In the same column, however, she included several other notices of social events, including a dinner party at which Mrs. J. W. Byrd "entertained a large number of her friends," a spend-the-day party given by Mrs. W. S. Hunter to which "a number of her lady friends were invited" to share "an elegant course dinner," and finally, an announcement that "today Mrs. James Thompson will entertain at an old-fashioned quilting, and her friends are anticipating the event with inexpressible pleasure." Stribling also noted that Al Thompson, the son of James and Lida Thompson, had spent the holidays with his "homefolks" before returning to a private school in Charlotte, and that Mrs. J. W. Byrd and sons and Miss Clara Hunt spent the weekend in Townville, a community some ten miles south of Seneca.[41] It appears to have been a busy week for these women.

Changing Roles for Women

Mattie Stribling's assessment that Mrs. Thompson's quilting "proved a happy climax to the many delightful social affairs of the holidays" takes on additional meaning when one sees it not only in the context of other such holiday gatherings but also as a follow-up to the heady

Old-Fashioned Quilting

public acclaim given the Blossom Show. Both the show and the quilting were opportunities for these women to perform in a public arena, the former directly, the latter vicariously through the newspaper narrative. The actions of these women during this period demonstrate the gradual transition for many women from the home-centered values, the "cult of domesticity," of the nineteenth century, to an extension of the women's sphere into areas of politics, social justice, mission work, and civic improvement in the early twentieth. Through participation in civic and religious organizations, women began "to redefine 'woman's place' by giving the concept a public dimension."[42] Participation in clubs and group activities during this period "gave an opportunity for middle-class women to find a new confidence, a voice (both literally and figuratively), and a vehicle for both personal and social development."[43]

Significance of an "Old-Fashioned Quilting"

The transformation and expansion of women's roles into a more public sphere during the early twentieth century was accompanied by friction. And the newspaper account of Mrs. Thompson's old-fashioned quilting provoked a particular response that provides an illustration of this tension. Mattie Stribling reported that, in setting the table in the manner of "ye day when quiltings were 'all the go,'" the hostess made use of a number of objects of family significance. These are described as "a nice fresh oil table cloth, . . . an heir loom of a hundred years," and as a centerpiece (what we would today call a table runner), "a square from a woven marseilles spread, . . . made by a relative of the family befo' de war," and "a tiny pitcher that was imported from across the water by a friend of the family, and dated back a hundred years." Stribling indicates that "these interesting facts" regarding the significance of the objects to the family were related by the hostess.

A week after this report, the *Keowee Courier* published the following item from another local correspondent:

> While in Seneca at the [Sunday School] convention we saw the Irish linen table cloth, referred to by your Seneca correspondent last week as having been used by Mrs. J. H. Thompson at her old-time quilting. The cloth is an

17

heirloom, having been used by Mrs. Thompson's grandmother, Mrs. James A. Doyle, long before the Civil War, and is now well preserved, being used only on state occasions. The home double-woven piece was woven by "Dilsey," a slave, who belonged to Mrs. James Doyle. These relics have been sacredly kept by Mrs. H. F. Alexander, who possesses high appreciation of relics of antiquity. The old spoon-holder used at this quilting was purchased in 1870. A china fruit bowl also used has been in the Alexander family 75 years, and the pitcher was presented to Mrs. Alexander by Mrs. Tidemann, of Charleston, in honor of her mother, who brought it from Germany. It is perhaps one hundred years old. . . . E. M. D.

The writer was Ella Dendy Doyle, the regular correspondent from the nearby Bountyland community. Her corrections to Mattie Stribling's descriptions of the objects convey a sense of indignation that the significance of such "sacred relics" had been misinterpreted or devalued. Not only did Stribling's report incorrectly identify the materials and construction of the two textile pieces and ignore two additional objects, but it lacked the proper reverential attitude toward the heirlooms. In her response, Ella Dendy Doyle demonstrated a nineteenth-century tendency to imbue objects with symbolic associations. According to Grier, "In Victorian culture, ordinary people used objects to create dense webs of connections to their culture and society."[44] Such objects make statements to others "that we actually are what our possessions claim us to be. They do this by being tied to chains of associative thought, both highly personal and conventional."[45]

For such families as the Dendys, Doyles, and Alexanders, the "chain of association" connected to these material objects was highly symbolic. Among the earliest settlers in what became Oconee County, these families defined their existence through their kinship networks, extensive rural land holdings, substantial homes, and inheritance, both tangible and intangible. For families who had lived through the tumult of the Civil War and Reconstruction, family heirlooms connected them with the perceived stability and gentility of the antebellum period. The invocation of the "holy city" of Charleston, the symbolic seat of South Carolina's antebellum heritage, caps Doyle's assertion of the exalted legacy of the Alexander family heirlooms.

In contrast, Lida Thompson inverted the meaning of the same hallowed objects by using them in association with a meager repast. In

Old-Fashioned Quilting

order to create a contrast with the social conventions of her own era—sumptuous refreshment and abundance—she ignored the conventional "chain of association" of the pre-war era with gentility, hospitality, and abundance. Instead, she evoked a past characterized as austere, rustic, and unrefined. By interpreting these objects in a different way than her parents and grandparents, Lida Alexander demonstrated a growing trend of the era. Some scholars have suggested that during the twentieth century, objects "were sometimes seen as one medium for articulating personality [rather] than formal cultural identity," as was more prevalent during the Victorian era, and that, "by the 1920s, cultural memory was not believed to reside in household possessions."[46]

Thus, one interpretation of Mrs. Thompson's "old-fashioned quilting" is that, along with the performance of "the Blossom Girls," the elaborate in-home entertainments of these women were part of an exploration of individual identity and participation with a peer group, and a move away from the collective identity provided by ancestry and objects of the past. From the newspaper accounts, Mrs. Thompson seems to have given a higher priority to enhancing her own reputation as a successful hostess than to honoring the values of her mother's family.

The contrast set up by Lida Thompson between the perceived rustic values of the past and the lavish gentility of her own day might also reflect the growing class divide among the white population resulting from the explosive growth of the textile industry in the upper South in the late-nineteenth and early-twentieth century. Poor white families left their tenant farms and flocked to textile mill villages in search of higher, more stable income. Townspeople carried ambivalent attitudes toward the mill workers. The success of commercial centers such as Seneca depended largely upon the textile trade; at the same time, the mill workers were both feared for their perceived lawlessness and derided for their uncultured behavior.[47] According to a study based on oral history interviews with mill workers, "As townsfolk created and refined their own standards of decorum, domesticity, and accumulation, they found themselves surrounded by workers whose way of life seemed increasingly alien."[48]

A number of newspaper items show how townspeople created par-

Uncoverings 2000

odies of stereotypical "poor white trash." On April 28, 1909, Mattie Stribling's column included an announcement for an upcoming "Harde Times Soshul":

> You air axed to a doins us folks air a goin to hav at the hum of Mr. and Mrs. J. T. Simpson. . . . Every woman who kums must ware a kaliker dress and apern, or somethin ekaly approperate, and leve their poughdle dorg to hum. . . . Gents must ware there old close and saft shirts. No gent with a biled shirt and dude koller will be aloud to kum unless he pays a fine of 5c. . . . A vote of thanks will be given to the man or woman hevin the worst lookin rig in the rume. Extry good eatins will be et from twilite to midnite. . . .Better kum—lots uv fun.[49]

The event was afterward reported by Mattie Stribling as "a big success, not the least of which is attributable to the efforts of the host and hostess to make it so. The lower floor of the house, including the parlor, hall, dining room and spacious piazzas, was literally turned over to the guests, and every thing was free and easy."[50] The judges for the costumes included J. H. Thompson, Lida's husband. The contrast between the hosts' large, elegant home and the rustic costume required of the guests mirrors the theme Mrs. Thompson created for her own guests some months later.

Newspaper writers frequently used representations of dialect to identify and stereotype groups by race or class. During the early twentieth century, the *Keowee Courier* frequently circulated jokes representing the stereotypic speech patterns of African Americans, Irish Americans, and poor whites. On September 15, 1909, the paper printed a long narrative about an actual social event, but which was framed as a fictional dialogue between two women regarding "Squire Crisp's Gal's Party." The dialogue was written in exaggerated Southern country dialect:

> "Good mornin', Sister Green. How be ye?"
>
> "Good mornin', Sister Turnipseed. I ain't feelin' much. I've got sich a mis'ry in me knee. 'Pears like it's goin' to be stiff, so I'm afeard it mought be this new distress—peg-leg-ry. What's the news with ye?"
>
> "La, bless ye! The weather's been so dry, there hain't no news, only the party down to 'Squire Crisp's t'other Wednesday night. . . .I wa'nt there, but I hearn all about it. . . ."[51]

Old-Fashioned Quilting

Pellagra, a debilitating disease resulting from a protein and vitamin deficiency, was a chronic problem in mill villages during the early twentieth century, especially for women and children. The disease is characterized by rough red blotches on the skin and general lethargy.[52] Both the reference to a disease affecting mill workers and the imitation of "poor white" speech patterns—demonstrate an attempt to define the social distance between Miss Annie Crisp's party-goers and the two fictional characters who were not invited.

Besides printing written representations of the dialects of lower-class groups for comic effect, newspaper writers also employed alternate spelling to indicate an event as "old-fashioned." An "old fashioned concerte" in Walhalla was organized in 1909 to benefit the Women's Civic Improvement Association. The program included "a big synge of ye old fashioned songes by all ye menne and womenne folkes with musick by ye old fiddle and guitar." While the invitation to this event does not use language to make associations with poverty in the same manner as the "hard times soshul," the orthography is intended to refer to an earlier time period when, it is supposed, people gathered in the town hall to sing old favorites such as "Old Folks at Home," "Flow Gently, Sweet Afton," and "Tenting on the Old Camp Ground."[53] Whether or not Lida Thompson used dialect in the performance of her "old-fashioned quilting," Mattie Stribling referred in her narrative to "ye day when quiltings were 'all the go'" and to the heirlooms which had been used by the family "befo' de war." The use of dialect is, again, intended to show the distance between the past and the present.

Mrs. Thompson's "old-fashioned quilting" did not occur as an isolated event. The hostess drew inspiration for her novel entertainment from other events taking place in the vicinity during the preceding months. She probably did not intend to offend her mother's friends by making sport with the family heirlooms, or to define the class distinctions between the gentility of her own social circle and the countrified ways of the men and women working in the local textile mills; however, the theme of her entertainment reflects the changing and conflicting values of the era.

Mrs. Thompson's quilting was not only the climax to the social affairs of the holidays, but also seems to have been the end of the published record of interactions among this particular group of eight women. During the next six months, there were no reports of meetings of the Every Tuesday Social Circle, no references to the Blossom Family, and no record of events at which more than one or two of the women were identified by name. Mrs. T. S. Stribling entertained the Ladies' Aid Society of the Presbyterian church, while Mrs. F. M. Cary hosted the Ladies' Missionary Society of the Baptist church. Mrs. T. E. Stribling rejoined the Once-A-Week Club. Mrs. J. W. Byrd and Mrs. J. H. Thompson traveled to Townville to assist with the wedding preparations for Miss Clara Hunt. Mrs. C. V. McCarey and Mrs. W. S. Hunter were involved in birthday parties and outings for their teenage children. On June 28, 1910, James H. Thompson's father, A. W. Thompson, died, and three months later the family moved to Atlanta. The "Local Matters About Seneca" columns during 1910 contain shorter accounts of social events and seem to lack the personality and inventiveness of earlier years. After June 15, 1910, the column no longer carried the familiar "M.V.S." signature, suggesting that some other, unidentified correspondent had taken over the Seneca beat.[54]

The newspaper item of Mrs. Thompson's quilting, along with the photograph taken by Nora Carver, document that on one particular day, eight women experienced a very enjoyable social event that included sitting around a quilt frame. The item does not suggest that this was a frequent activity for these participants; on the contrary, the implication is that quilting was part of an evocation of the past, designed to demonstrate that the hostess and her guests were women of a new, progressive, refined era in contrast to an "old-fashioned" agrarian kinship network.

The early decades of the twentieth century represent an important transitional era, during which there were great transformations in women's roles, local and regional economic structures, and mass communications. Yet there have been surprisingly few studies of quiltmaking practices between the crazy-quilt era of the late-nineteenth century and the growing influence of the urban-centered Colonial Revival during the twentieth.

This study of the significance of a single quilting event suggests that there are many possible levels of involvement and many possible motivations—some of them personal, some of them social—for participating in quiltmaking activity. The context for a single event can be very complex. Quilt researchers tend to focus attention on groups and individuals for whom quilts are an important part of their identities. As this study suggests, there is also much to be learned about individuals who are not active quiltmakers but who use quilts casually to achieve personal or social goals.

Notes and References

1. "Local Matters About Seneca," *Keowee Courier*, hereinafter cited as *KC*, 12 January 1910. Subsequent quotations from this item appear in italics to distinguish them from other quotations.

2. This item was one of a number of published narratives located during a search for references to quilts, quiltmakers, or quilting events. Although there were other mentions of quiltmaking activity, the item describing Mrs. Thompson's quilting was the most intriguing.

3. U.S. Bureau of the Census, *1910 Federal Census, Supplement for South Carolina*.

4. For more information on women's organizations, see Anne Firor Scott, *Natural Allies: Women's Associations in American History* (Urbana: University of Illinois Press, 1991); and Theodora Penny Martin, *The Sound of Our Own Voices: Women's Study Clubs, 1860–1910* (Boston: Beacon Press, 1987).

5. Scott, 80.

6. Beverly Gordon, "Victorian Fancywork in the American Home: Fantasy and Accommodation," in Marilyn Ferris Motz and Pat Browne, eds., *Making the American Home: Middle-Class Women and Domestic Material Culture, 1840–1940* (Bowling Green, OH: Bowling Green State University Popular Press, 1988), 48.

7. "Local and Personal," *KC*, 31 March 1909.

8. Martin, 118–19.

9. The Sunshine Society was founded in New York City in 1896 by Cynthia Westover Alden. The Society's mission was "to incite its members to the performance of kind and helpful deeds, and to thus bring the sunshine of happiness into the greatest possible number of hearts and homes." In 1909, nine local Sunshine Societies were reported in Oconee County, with a membership of 268 men and women. Frederic Haskin, "International Sunshine," *KC*, 18 August 1909; Julia D. Shanklin, "The Sunshine Work," *KC*, 28 July 1909.

10. *KC*, various issues, 1909–1910.

11. For comparative information on quilting events reported in newspapers, see Kari Ronning, "Quilting in Webster County, Nebraska, 1880–1920, in *Uncoverings 1992*, ed. Laurel Horton (San Francisco: American Quilt Study Group, 1993), 169–91.

12. Katherine C. Grier, "The Decline of the Memory Palace: The Parlor after 1890," in Jessica H. Foy and Thomas Schlereth, eds., *American Home Life, 1880–*

1930: A Social History of Spaces and Services (Knoxville: University of Tennessee Press, 1992), 53–54.

13. "Local Matters About Seneca," hereinafter cited as "Seneca Matters," *KC*, 24 March 1909.

14. Other social events during this time were also described as "old-fashioned," including charity quiltings in Fair Play community (*KC*, 15 December 1909) and Richland community (*KC*, 26 October 1910), and an "old-fashioned concerte" [sic] sponsored by the Women's Civic Improvement Association of Walhalla (*KC*, 7 July 1909).

15. Frances Holleman, *The City of Seneca, South Carolina, The City of Opportunity: Its Centennial, 1873–1973* (Greenville, SC: Creative Printers, 1973), 133.

16. Virginia Gunn to author, correspondence, 30 January 1998.

17. Holleman, 52.

18. U.S. Bureau of the Census, *1910 Federal Census, State of South Carolina, Oconee County*; hereinafter cited as *1910 Census*; Holleman, 31, 71, 133, 163; *KC*, 6 April 1910. On September 24, 1910, the Thompson family left Seneca "to make their future home" in Atlanta. "Seneca Items," *Spartanburg Herald*, 25 September, 1910.

19. *1910 Census*; Holleman, 14, 62, 74, 133, 150, 168.

20. *1910 Census*; Holleman, 51, 62, 70, 133, 150, 195.

21. *1910 Census*; Holleman, 133, 163.

22. Sonnie Magee herself apparently had worked as a schoolteacher before her marriage, as there is evidence of a tuition receipt dated 1897 with her signature. *1910 Census*; Holleman, 31, 40, 49, 50, 60, 61, 86, 133, 150.

23. *1910 Census*; Holleman, 48, 86, 133.

24. *1910 Census*; Holleman, 71, 133, 159.

25. *1910 Census*; Holleman, 133, 171; 190; Bruce Hodgson Stribling, *Striblings of Walnut Hill and Related Families* (Greenville, SC: Keys Printing Co., 1979), 37–46; "Seneca Matters," *KC*, 6 April 1910.

26. "Seneca Matters," *KC*, 27 October 1909.

27. Seneca Presbyterian Church Membership Roll; *Oconee County, South Carolina, Cemetery Survey*, Vol. 1 (Greenville, SC: A Press, 1983).

28. David L. Carlton, *Mill and Town in South Carolina, 1880–1920* (Baton Rouge: Louisiana State University Press, 1982), 22–23.

29. Holleman, 126.

30. There is no record that Mrs. J. H. Thompson, Mrs. T. S. Stribling, or Mrs. J. F. Alexander ever were members of the Once-A-Week Club. The latter two women, ages fifteen and twenty-two respectively, were unmarried in 1896. Once-A-Week Club, *Minutes*, Books One and Two (1896–1915), Special Collections, Clemson University Library.

31. Holleman, 133.

32. "Seneca Matters," *KC*, 17 February 1909, 1.

33. Ibid., 20 October 1909. Additional references to an earlier production of the "Blossom Show" have not been located.

34. Ibid., 17 November 1909,1.

35. Ibid.

Old-Fashioned Quilting

36. Ibid., 1 December 1909, 1.
37. Holleman, 62.
38. "Seneca Matters," *KC*, 15 December 1909, 1.
39. Ibid., 29 December 1909.
40. "Local News," *Farm and Factory*, 4 January 1910. Befitting Seneca's role as a new commercial center, this newspaper published more items of concern to business and trade than the *Keowee Courier*.
41. "Seneca Matters," *KC*, 5 January 1910.
42. Scott, 2.
43. Karen J. Blair, *The Torchbearers: Women and their Amateur Arts Association in America, 1890–1930* (Bloomington: Indiana University Press, 1994), 31.
44. Grier, 56.
45. Ibid., 54–56.
46. Ibid., 68–69.
47. Carlton, 145–50.
48. Jacquelyn Dowd Hall, et al., *Like a Family: The Making of a Southern Cotton Mill World* (Chapel Hill: University of North Carolina Press, 1987), 132.
49. "Seneca Matters," *KC*, 28 April 1909.
50. Ibid., 5 May 1909.
51. "Squire Crisp's Gal's Party," *KC*, 15 September 1909.
52. Hall, 132.
53. "Old Fashioned Concerte," *KC*, 7 July 1909.
54. *KC*, 23 February, 13 April, 2 March, 22 June, 13 July, and 16 March 1910.

Textiles and Cooperative Commerce in Colonial America: The Example of William McCormick

Xenia E. Cord

Based on an unpublished, handwritten account book maintained by William McCormick from 1751 through 1782, this research reconstructs the life of a Virginian in southwestern Pennsylvania who prospered by cooperative commerce. Trained as a weaver of linen goods, McCormick practiced this craft when necessary, also establishing himself as a frontiersman, ranger, and teamster hauling commodities between Winchester, Virginia, and Fort Pitt. He was responsible for considerable textile production during the Revolution, when provisioning volunteer militia was the responsibility of the community. Bartering yardages for commodities and cooperative labor was an integral part of the sustenance of any frontier community. The medium of exchange was the value each participant placed on his own labor and skills, and the acceptance of that value by others. The manuscript contains many names of those with whom McCormick did business, requiring extensive search in colonial census materials to determine the locations, relationships, and nature of these associations.

Cooperative labor has long been a traditional form of commerce, and was vital to the developing frontier areas of the American colonies. During the mid-1760s and for the next decade, England's Parliament virtually assured the need for the barter system in the colonies. Perhaps nowhere was this pattern more clear than on the frontier of western Pennsylvania, comprising as it did the westernmost reaches of Anglo-European colonial settlement. The geographic conditions of the region, combined with economic problems created by law, weather, and political uncertainty demanded that trade be carried out almost without currency or imported items. These conditions and others are well illustrated in a manuscript account book belonging to one William McCormick, Virginian by birth, Scotch-Irish and nominal Anglican by heritage, southwestern Pennsylvania frontiersman, teamster, soldier, and sometime weaver of linen goods.[1]

Little has been published about the conduct of business by the men who wove linen in America in the preindustrial era. Domestic weaving of linen fabrics was commonly done by women; indeed, in the decade leading up to the Revolution it became a distaff accomplishment encouraged by patriotism and in some colonies required by law.[2] It was not until 1797 that the first machinery for the wholesale manufacturing of linen was introduced on the western Pennsylvania frontier, although in New England earlier attempts had been made to initiate mass production of linen textiles.[3] The laborious and time-consuming steps necessary to produce linen yarn from standing flax, and then to complete the process of making natural or bleached linen, precluded mechanical methods of production until long after the Revolution. By the time technology had created a practical way, vastly expanded cultivation of cotton had provided a cheaper, simpler, and more accessible raw material for textile manufacturing. But until that time, there existed a class of men who made a business of producing linen by handicraft, using for the most part yarn spun by others, and receiving in compensation not cash, but goods and in-kind payments.[4]

So pervasive has been the domestic manufacture of linen in America's history that household textile items (and their storage place) are still collectively referred to as "linens," although most of those articles are made of other fibers today. And "heirloom" suggests the value historically assigned to woven textiles. Durable linen cloth, if not made into garments, had a long life and was frequently recycled. Some eighteenth-century quilters chose linen sheets as the surface for their appliqué designs, or used them as quilt backings.[5]

It appears likely that flax was the first non-food crop planted in new settlement areas. Broadly and thickly sowed, the closeness of the plants produced a superior slender stalk and kept down weeds. After the long growing season, farmers pulled the plants from the ground and threshed out the seeds for subsequent crops or for sale. The plants were stored for later processing or sunk in a pond to break down the woody stems. The plants could also be piled on a platform with a fire beneath to dry the stems and make them brittle. Processors first crushed bundles of stems in a flax break, then scraped them with a wooden tool called a scutching knife, and then pulled them through a series of ever-finer combs to remove the outer husks. The supple strands growing within the tough, woody stems were extracted and spun to make yarn, which was then woven into linen fabric.[6] The preparation was lengthy and labor-intensive, alleviated only by cooperative labor.

In the central and northern colonies, and especially in their western reaches, people depended on leather garments or on previously acquired articles of clothing. It was not uncommon for owners to will items of dress to specific heirs, so great was the premium attached to manufactured fabric, especially if imported.[7] The cultivation of flax and the production of linen, tow, and linsey-woolsey eased somewhat the need for manufactured clothing or fabric from England, although the domestic fabric was generally accounted inferior to that which could be imported. Nonetheless, on the frontier it was at a premium and welcomed accordingly, and in fact seems to have been of an excellent and serviceable quality.

By the time the western parts of present-day Pennsylvania were officially opened to settlement in 1768, residents of the colonies had been engaged in individual efforts at flax production for over 150 years. Economic necessity had dictated this personal industry; in the mid-1760s, however, politics also began to affect domestic textile production, including linen. England had consistently maintained a policy of discouraging any industry in its colonies which would offer competition to its own manufactories and upset its favorable balance of trade. Colonial territories were exploited for their raw materials. In exchange the colonies might anticipate a monopolistic market, a ready supply of manufactured goods (at competitive prices), and such governmental and military paternalism as the crown could conveniently and advantageously supply.

In 1763 nearly seventy years of territorial conflict with France had been concluded with the Treaty of Paris, but the war had drained the royal treasury. A large part of that expense had been occasioned by the necessity of sending British troops to North America to fight the French and their Indian allies, and to defend English colonists. British military leadership was often unequal to the task of war in the new world; it relied upon standards of traditional warfare, was unable to make good use of colonial fighting techniques similar to those of the Indian enemy, and suffered costly losses.[8]

With the cessation of hostilities Parliament determined to consolidate its colonial administration, underwriting the cost of military preparedness with a series of revenue acts. Imports to the American colonies were taxed and regulated; hard currency was required in payment. With little to export, the commodity-poor New England colonies engaged in a triangular trade, selling Caribbean rum and sugar in England and carrying slaves from Africa to the Caribbean. The Southern colonies, where producers and shippers of raw materials frequently incurred debts well beyond the value of their exports, were also required to pay for imported goods in real money. Colonial governments were forbidden to create paper money as legal tender for debts, and new taxes were levied requiring the purchase of tax stamps for all printed matter, including books, business transactions, legal documents, and newspapers. When additional import duties on such disparate items as fabrics, glass, paper, and tea were imposed, the merchant class in much of colonial America, joined by political malcontents and patriotic citizens alike, voted to boycott imported goods and to use instead items of their own manufacture.[9]

The colonial experience was not entirely one of nationalism growing toward independence, with the Revolution as the culmination of that spirit. In fact most colonists had local and familial loyalties, and their political focus was confined in general to government issues in their home colony only. But as Englishmen they were accustomed to certain rights under a monarchy, including the expectation of representation in Parliament by elected or hereditary members from their district. In the American colonies these rights were restricted by economic policies established in London, far from the places where application of the policies resulted in conflict.

On the frontier, where currency was already in very short supply and where necessity and geography dictated that subsistence items be locally produced, the limitations imposed by Parliament may not have had much economic effect. What the several public responses to the taxation acts did was to bring into alignment the economies in general use in frontier areas with the "sacrifices" being made on principle in eastern settled areas. Linen became an important commodity on which the boycott focused, largely because it was a product which could be produced by many individual efforts in a public display of solidarity.

As soon as the boycott on imported textiles was announced, patriotic fervor demanded a generous response. Public spinning and weaving contests were held, with prizes going to those who produced the greatest volume of linen on the spot, or to those whose output was the greatest over a given period.[10] The senior class of Harvard announced, in 1768, that at commencement all would appear dressed only in homespun garments.[11] Rolla Tryon, in *Household Manufactures in the United States, 1640–1860*, quoted from one contemporary source that "each family vigorously to [sic] set about to manufacturing their own cloathing, and every other necessary article. . . . At another gentleman's house where I was, his lady was spinning fast, and had five clever girls spinning along with her . . . they will soon have a good deal of cloth to sell."[12] Another source from May 1768 reported that "one married lady and her daughter of about sixteen, have spun full sixty yards of good fine linen cloth, nearly a yard wide, since the first of March."[13]

Carl Bridenbaugh, in *The Colonial Craftsman*, noted that by 1750 nine-tenths of the farmers in Pennsylvania produced their own clothing textiles, and quoted a Philadelphia merchant as saying:

> A vast deal of linen and woolen is made within the Province; so much linen by the back Irish inhabitants that they not only hawk a great deal frequently about both town and country, but they carry considerable quantities away to the Eastward by land, quite as far away as Rhode Island.[14]

Throughout the colonies, individuals reasserted their independence from goods of British manufacture, and perhaps nowhere with greater effect than in the manufacture of domestic textiles.

Among the settlers of the colonies for whom the manufacture of linen and other fabrics was a craft were the Scotch-Irish, who migrated in several waves in the early and middle 1700s. This group included numerous weavers who were a part of the great Irish tradition of linen weaving, and in the colonies they found a ready market for their skills. A great many Scotch-Irish immigrated to the Shenandoah Valley of Virginia, enticed by the promise of cheap land and by an imaginative immigration system operated by James Patton, an agent for William Beverley. More than two dozen times Patton made trips to Ireland in his ship, carrying tobacco, skins, and other colonial produce to the mother country, and bringing Ulstermen back with him. Many of them settled on a 1736 grant comprising 118,491 acres in the Shenandoah Valley.[15]

Among the earliest Scotch-Irish into the area was Dr. John McCormick, a graduate of the University of Dublin, who moved from Pennsylvania to Virginia about 1734 with Joist Hite. The surveys of the land were done by George Washington, and Dr. McCormick supposedly carried the survey chains. By 1740 McCormick had built on his acreage a stone house which served as both showplace and fortification for his area.[16] He and his wife Ann McFarren McCormick were the parents of eight children, most of them born at Summit Hill, near Winchester, in Virginia colony. Their son William was born there in 1738.[17]

If William's literacy is any proof, the doctor's children received some sort of regular education and learned at least to read, write, and cipher. His spelling was often creative and reflected the Scotch-Irish speech patterns around him, but his math skills were equal to the task of accurate accounting. When he was twelve, William was apprenticed to a weaver, possibly his uncle James McCormick, to learn that craft. There is evidence that a weaver operated in Winchester about this time: in the will of Ann Hollingsworth of Winchester, written March 2, 1748 and probated April 5, 1749, she bequeathed to her son George "a piece of cloth that was made betweixt [sic] me and my son Isaac, my son George paying for the weaving," and to her two married daughters, Margaret Carter and Lydia Neill, "a quantity of linen yarn I have at the weaver's."[18]

At the time of his apprenticeship or for his twelfth birthday, William was presented with a fine leather-bound account book, in which he entered his business transactions for more than thirty years (see figure 1). The account book is four inches by six inches, bound in leather which is still supple today, and which was at one time dyed a brilliant green. The binding is stitched, and the quarto-sized pages bear

Textiles and Cooperative Commerce

Figure 1. William McCormick's "pockit book" measures 4" x 6" x 1" thick. When the flap is lifted, faint traces of green dye are still evident on the leather. The clasp, although incomplete, shows marks of having been hand tooled, and the pages are still firmly stitched together. Private collection.

the watermark of John Whatman of Kent, giving some indication of the book's approximate date of manufacture and place of origin.[19] The book has a brass clasp, and the pages are ruled for accounting. The bulk of the entries occurred between 1765 and 1780; for some reason not apparent, William entered accounts from both ends of the book, one end upside down.

The earliest entry in William McCormick's "pockit book" is March 16, 1751, when William was thirteen (see figure 2). James McCormick is listed as "deter" (debtor), his debt consisting of fifteen shillings owed for the weaving of thirty yards of "Lining" (linen) at six pence per yard. Again in March and early in April he incurred further debts of £1 for thirty-three yards of linen at seven pence per yard, and twenty yards at six pence. On April first William received for his labors two shillings, six pence worth of linen yardage, and one shilling's worth of "grubb," suggesting a supportive and instructional relationship with James McCormick. Later he also received in cash one dollar, and an unspecified debt of £1.7.0 was paid to Jonathan Lupton on his behalf.

The only other entry in the book in the 1750s was when young William paid for thirty-four half pints of some beverage, at a total of ten shillings, seven and a half pence, for a debt incurred by "Mr. Mansfeeld" while gaming at "Mr. Hareson's" on February 12, 1752. Perhaps Mr. Harrison made amends to the fourteen-year-old William, for it does not appear that Mr. Mansfield ever repaid the bill. The gaming mentioned by William at that early date was the first in a long series of gambling and other pleasures in which he participated. Throughout the book he recorded his own or others' expenses for playing cribbage, racing horses, attending a "ball alley" and a "club," pitching (horseshoes?), playing "fives" (a game similar to handball played on a three or four- sided court), playing cards and "swango" (not identified further), and drinking a variety of intoxicants from cider to sangre, much of which William supplied. Reverend William McClure, an itinerant preacher who in 1772 visited the vicinity of Fort Pitt where William was living, observed:

> The manners of the people of Virginia, who have removed into these parts, are different from those of the presbyterians and germans. They are much addicted to drinking parties, gambling, horse race & fighting. They are hospitable & prodigal.[20]

Although the preacher would hardly have mentioned it, visiting houses of ill repute was also apparently a part of the entertainment enjoyed by young Virginia gentlemen. Such a visit caused William at least one painful infection, if the "song" he penned in commemoration of the event is any indication. Wryly humorous, the verses lament his gullibility in believing his assignation to be with a virgin, and mention several remedies then popularly believed to be efficacious in the treatment of social diseases. William's sporting activities and forthright verses suggest that those with aristocratic aspirations in Virginia, and those trans-Appalachian Scotch-Irish Anglicans, were less concerned for their moral welfare and their mortal souls than were their neighboring colonists in Pennsylvania and New England.

After his apprenticeship ended sometime between 1757 and 1760, William McCormick seems to have combined his weaving occupation with a more peripatetic lifestyle. With the whole wilderness of North America at his doorstep, he could hardly be faulted for not wanting to spend his life indoors, tied to a loom. By 1762 he was also engaged in trading or teamstering, apparently bringing in goods from the East Coast to the Winchester area and bartering them, while receiving in trade items which might be sold in the East, either in Williamsburg or Baltimore.

Also in 1762 McCormick made the first entry for William Crawford, a neighbor who became a close personal friend and eventually William's father-in-law. Crawford, a Virginian six or seven years McCormick's senior, was a factor for George Washington, representing Washington's vast real estate holdings in western Pennsylvania. Virginia exercised its colonial prerogative by claiming all of the land to its west, as far as the land extended, and by some fluke of political geography this included a large portion of southwestern Pennsylvania.[21] Crawford moved to the area south of British-controlled Fort Pitt in 1766, settling on the west bank of the Youghiogheny River. He encouraged many of his Virginia neighbors and their families, including William McCormick, to accompany him to the new settlement area.[22]

By 1766 McCormick had established a trade route into the area of Fort Pitt, on the western frontier.[23] His account book reveals that he had a steady business bringing salt, iron for horseshoes, buttons, buckles, and seed to the west, and bringing out the skins of bears, deer, elk,

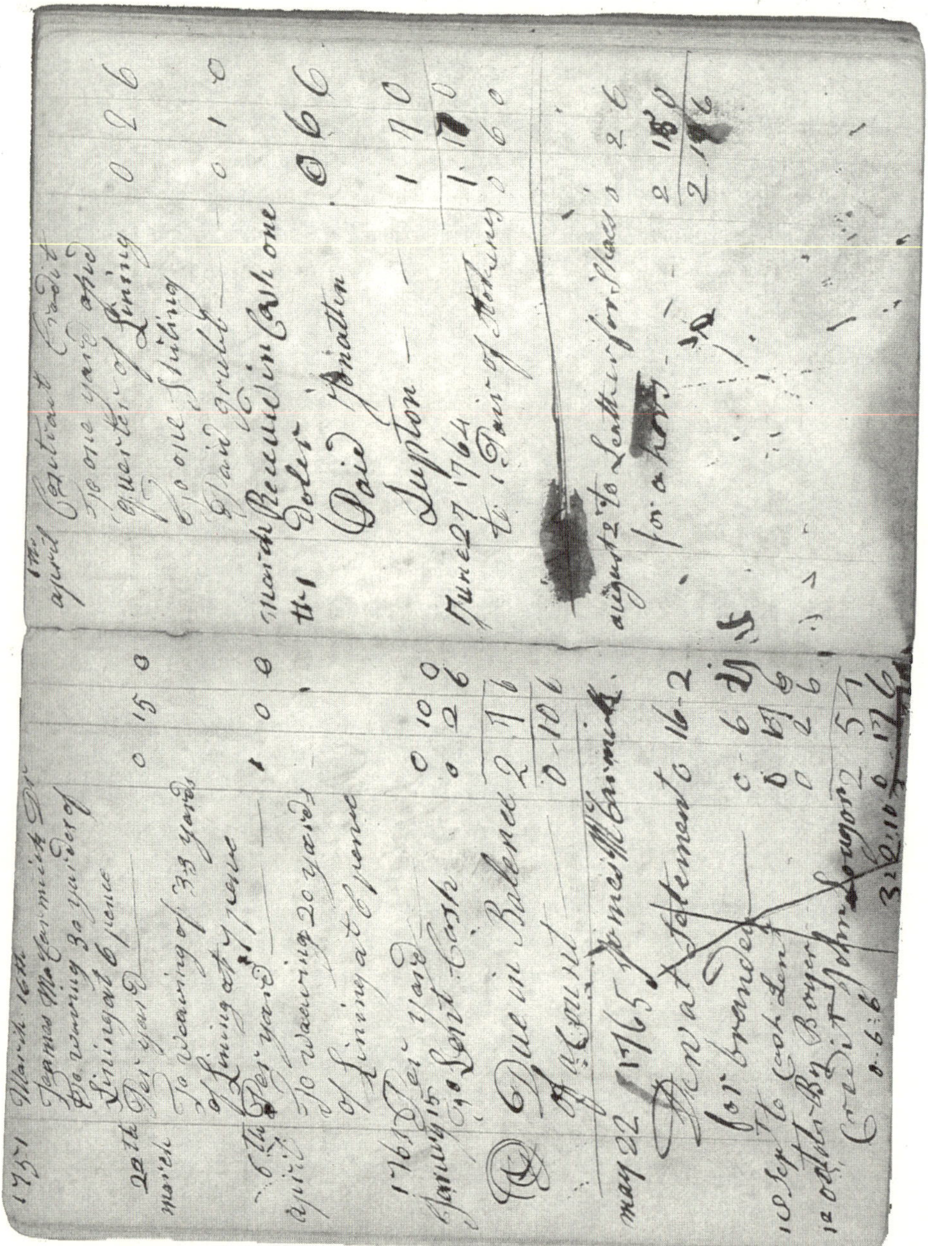

Textiles and Cooperative Commerce

Figure 2. The earliest entry in the account book:

1751	March 16 James McCormick Dr [debtor]			1st April	Contract Credit	
	To weaving 30 yards of lining [linen] at 6 pence per yard	0.15.0			To one yard aprd[?] quarter of lining	0.2.6
22th March	To weaving of 33 yards of Lining at 7 pence per yard	1.0.0		March the 1	To one shiling paid grubb Received in cash one Dolar	0.1.0 0.6.6
6th April	To weaving 20 yards of Lining at 6 pence per yard	0.10.0			Paid Jonathen Lupton	1.7.0
1763 January 15	To lent cash	0.2.6		June 27 1764	To 1 pair of Moksines [moccasins]	0.6.0
	Due in Balance of Account	2.7.6 0.10.6		August 2	To leather for shoes for a hors [horse]	0.2.6 2.15.0 2.17.6

May 22 1765 James McCormick
         Dew at Satement [sic]
         for brandy   0.16.2
18 Sept to cash lent   0.6.8
12 October By Boyer   0.67.3
Credit John Lougon   0.2.6
         0.6.6   3.2.10   2.5.4
                                           0.17.6

37

otters, panthers, and raccoons, brains used for curing hides, occasional scalps (on which the government paid a bounty), and other frontier products (see figure 3).[24]

The entries in McCormick's book are generally brief, sometimes with more than one account per page, and feature such items as boots, brandy, and buttons, with livestock and hides for payment. Also among the debts are entries for whiskey and other alcoholic beverages, grain, gunpowder, seeds, salt, textiles, and tools; he was often owed for long periods of time, and must have been willing to carry the debts. Gambling is a common entry, and cash payments were often made in local currency, of which there were several kinds. Entries include notations of (possibly Spanish) dollars, pounds, shillings and pence, and "Pennsylvania money." William's practice was to transpose all debts into English coinage and to record them in pounds, shillings, and pence regardless of their original denominations.

It is difficult to assess the importance, nature, and variety of commerce conducted by William McCormick; he appears to have been a man who prospered by the opportunities in the wilderness around him, and by conditions created by the economic and political climate of his time. It is tempting to recreate the rhythm of his days; it is possible, based on his account book, to see the pattern of opportunities upon which he capitalized.

The cooperative labor system into which William McCormick fit as a trader moving between frontier and civilization was one based on kinship and long-standing friendship, not on necessity and desperation. By 1768, when the death of his father in Virginia required his attention in settling the estate, William was moving constantly between the eastern settlements and the "Yough" region of western Pennsylvania, and had assumed some responsibility for his brother Andrew, who was traveling with him. By this time the settlement in what is now Fayette County, Pennsylvania, included many members of families who had lived in the Winchester, Virginia, area. Among them were the families of William Crawford's brother Valentine, at least two of their five Stephenson half-brothers, Crawford's brother-in-law John Vance, McCormick's brothers James, John, George, and Andrew, and a cousin Oliver, and other former residents of the Winchester area.

By 1770 McCormick had established a farm in Fayette County,

Textiles and Cooperative Commerce

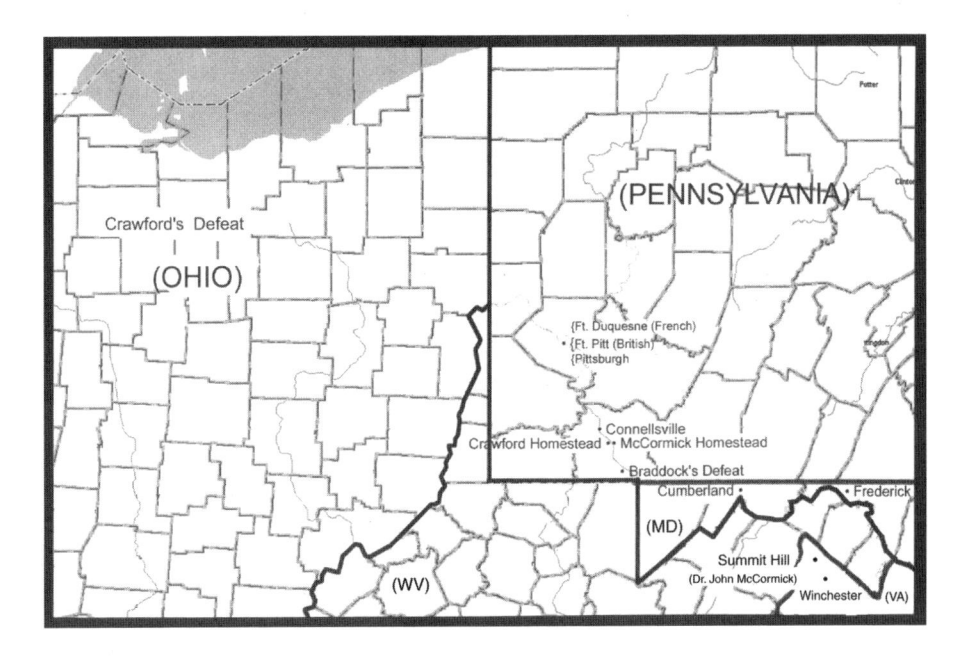

Figure 3. Map of the Upper Ohio Valley in the eighteenth century, showing the location of principal towns and places of significance in the McCormick manuscript. Present-day county and state lines are also shown.

planting rye, and sisal, and wheat, and enabling neighbors to repay their debts to him by harvesting his crops. He also raised flax and corn, and kept hogs. During this time he formed an attachment for Effelica "Effie" Crawford, daughter of his friend William Crawford. Even without William's notation (twice) in his account book of the date of their marriage, it is possible to see the preparations William was making for Effie's comfort, and to interpret their meaning. By 1772 McCormick was beginning to accumulate belongings that spoke of permanency, and this accumulation was done by the system of cooperation.

Although no notation appears in the book, sometime before April 1772 McCormick built a single-pen log house on the eastern side of the Youghioheny River, directly across from William Crawford's home. In January of that year he had provided James Willis with flaxseed, pork, and corn, and in return Willis built him a "stoon chimbley" for the new house, doing the work in April (see figure 4). The previous October William had brought salt and wheat seed to John Daw-

39

kins, who in June repaid William by crafting two windows and two doors for the new house (see figure 5). Brother George McCormick, whose business with William was mostly in cash loans, partially repaid his debts in 1772 by supplying two pots and a dough trough used for making yeast bread, probably handmade for Effie (see figure 6). In 1776 William supposedly replaced or expanded the home to a double pen, consisting of two rooms with a central hall and continuous roof, and two chimneys, which was still standing late in the nineteenth century.[25]

Later in 1772 William called upon the skills of another local craftsman, John Dickson. McCormick had in September brought Dickson a spoke shave, chisel, and a drawing knife, and had paid for some metal work, and in return Dickson built William a wagon (see figure 7). Because road conditions to the east would not support wagon travel, it is likely this vehicle was for local use, and indicated William's intent to intensify his local business and to cut back on his long and frequent trips out of the area. And by May 1773 his account book shows he was weaving again.

On February 18, 1773 William and Effie were married. While no account of the ceremony exists, contemporary writings give an idea of the sort of event it must have been. Reverend David McClure's account of a wedding in a "settlement of Virginians, near Yohiogeni" two months earlier suggests the style of William and Effie's wedding:

> [December] 17. Attended a marriage, where the guests were all Virginians. It was a scene of wild and confused merriment. The log house which was large, was filled. They were dancing to the music of a fiddle. They took little or no notice of me, on my entrance.
>
> After setting a while at the fire, I arose and desired the music and dancing to cease, & requested the Bride and Bridegroom to come forward. They came snickering and very merry. I desired the company who still appeared to be very mirthful & noisy, to attend with becoming seriousness, the solemnity.
>
> As soon as the ceremony was over, the music struck up, and the dancing was renewed. The Lady of a Mr. Stevenson, sent her husband to me, with her compliments requesting me to dance a minuit with her. My declining the honor, on the principle that was unacquainted with it, was scarcely accepted. He still politely urged, until I totally refused. After supper I rode about three miles to the house of a friend.[26]

Textiles and Cooperative Commerce

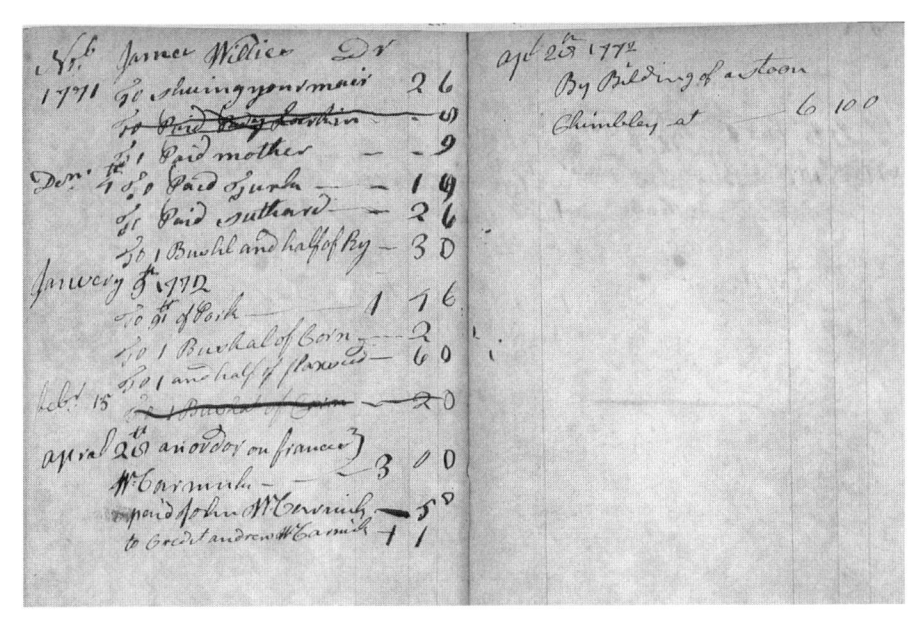

Figure 4. Complicated debts paid on behalf of James Willis to "mother," Francis McCormick, and John McCormick to credit Andrew McCormick, and purchases of supplies put Willis in debt to William McCormick. This account was apparently paid in full by the building of a "stoon chimbley" valued at 6.10.0. The spelling hints at McCormick's pattern of speech.

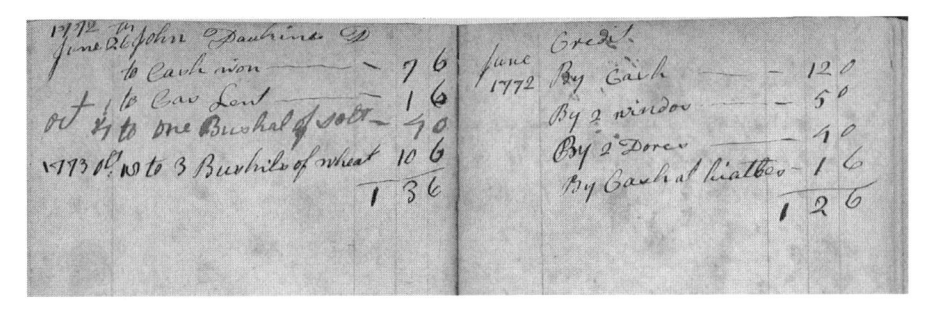

Figure 5. John Dawkins was in debt to McCormick over gambling, a loan, and the purchase of salt and wheat. He repaid nearly the entire amount at once, with cash and labor, building 2 doors and 2 windows for McCormick's log house.

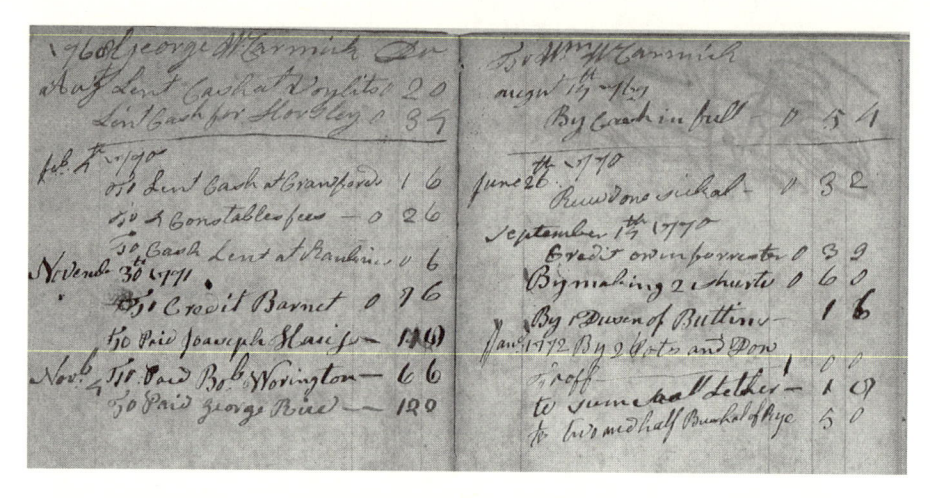

Figure 6. McCormick's brother George seems to have borrowed freely from him, and allowed William to pay debts on his behalf. In repayment George did farm labor, made 2 shirts and provided a dozen buttons, and in January 1772 gave his brother "2 Pots and Dow Troff," apparently wedding gifts for Effie Crawford.

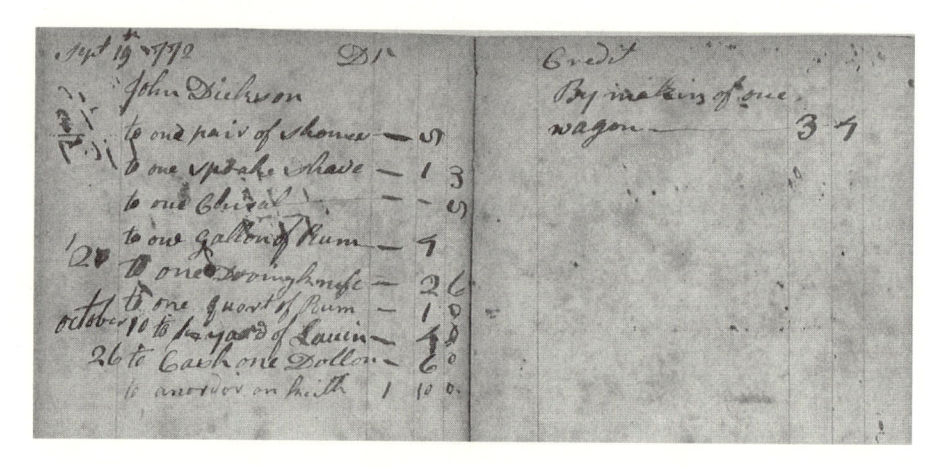

Figure 7. Provided with a spoke shave, a chisel, a drawing knife, and "an order on smith" [possibly metal wheel rims], John Dickson was well supplied with the tools he needed to repay his debt by making a wagon for McCormick.

While this wedding was not William and Effie's it may have been one of either family or friends; the "Lady" referred to was probably the wife of one of Effie's Stephenson half-uncles.

By the time armed conflict broke out between the colonies and Great Britain in 1775, William McCormick seems to have sharply curtailed his teamstering activities. Several factors may have accounted for this. The trade embargoes enforced by eastern merchants severely limited the value of goods from the interior that might have been exported, among them furs, hides, and flaxseed for Ireland.[27] Without a market abroad for these products, trade with the East would not have been as profitable for McCormick. While the western settlements may still have needed commodities from the East, they also had less purchasing power there. Too, the slowly developing civilization on the frontier made certain commodities more locally available. Salt, for instance, was now obtainable from several Kentucky sites that had before been in dangerous wilderness, and coal and iron ore had been discovered in great quantities locally, although the technology for their full utilization had not been developed. Flax was being grown in the Yough in much greater amounts, since English fabric was no longer available even to those who could afford it. And although few people were killed by Indians in the Yough region, alarms were common and forts were built every few miles; this threat may also have contributed to McCormick's making less frequent trips east.[28]

On January 23, 1775, the Pennsylvania provincial convention met to resolve certain measures concerning its boycott of British goods, and in order to provide for a domestic supply to replace them. The convention decided that sheep under four years should not be butchered, but raised instead for the wool they produced, and that manufactures of wool items such as "coating, flannel, blankets, rugs or coverlids, hosiery and coarse cloths both broad and narrow" be established, and required that anyone having the land must raise enough hemp and flax for personal use and for surplus. Salt, iron for nails and wire, steel, paper, glass, malt liquors and other items were discussed and their immediate manufacture resolved. Paper production was dependent on a supply of cloth, so the convention requested "the people of this province, in their respective houses, . . . order the necessary steps be taken for preserving these otherwise useless articles [old linen and woolen rags]." The convention recommended a factory for making wool combs and cards, customarily bought from other colonies, and suggested that "premiums ought to be granted in the several counties to persons who may excel in the several branches of manufactory." Finally, it forbid profit-taking under penalty of attainder.[29]

By the following year the provincial congress of Pennsylvania had initiated action on the establishment of military units. Pennsylvania was to provide the continental army with six thousand militia, who were to be supplied with "arms, accoutrements and camp kettles" by the county from which they came, or else the same were to be lent for the duration of the action, and returned to the province when the militia was disbanded. According to the Clothier General of the Army's account in 1781, noncommissioned officers and privates were to have a regimental coat, vest, breeches, overalls, a hat, two pairs each of hose, socks and linen overalls, four pairs of shoes, a pair of gloves, a pair of shoe buckles, a blanket, a rifle frock, and one stock clasp, at a total cost of $34.00. But when the war began, uniforms were not uniform, and most soldiers supplied their own.[30]

Among those who raised battalions were William Crawford and his son-in-law William Harrison. The provisioning of their troops is evident in the accounts of William McCormick, who had begun to address the profitable business of providing fabrics in answer to the boycott of British goods. In 1776 he wove, from linen yarn supplied him from the women of the neighborhood, about 550 yards of fabric. Most of this fabric was linen and linsey; some of it was the coarser hemp and tow fabrics, and a very small portion specialty items like striped material and handkerchief linen. By far the two largest customers were Crawford and Harrison. As family and as military men answering the colony's call, these men would have had first claim on McCormick's time and talent. A biographical sketch of Crawford says that "upon the news of the battle of Lexington, he at once raised and equipped a regiment for the defense of the colonies; this not being at the time accepted, he was on the 14th of August, 1776, commissioned as colonel of the Seventh Regiment Virginia Battalions."[31] Crawford's actions on behalf of Virginia in the short-lived "Lord Dunmore's War" while an officer of the Pennsylvania courts made a Pennsylvania commission unlikely. The regiment he raised served from Pennsylvania, but Crawford was obliged to turn to Virginia for a commission.

For 1776, William McCormick's account book records almost nothing but entries for weaving, and the various ways in which this work was repaid (see table 1). Crawford paid entirely in cash, while Harrison and others paid in commodities, including finished linen fabric. Most of the business seems to have been conducted with men of William's acquaintance, who must have conducted business for their wives, for it was the women and children in the family who spun the flax into yarn. All clothing was of course constructed by hand, again by the women of the community. On the few occasions when a page in his account book bears a woman's name, it may be because she had no adult male to do business for her. He dealt with the Widow Harrison, probably William Harrison's mother and the widow of Lawrence, whom McCormick had known since childhood; he dealt with Ann Connell, wife of Captain James, and sister of William's wife Effie; he dealt with Sukie Lyons and with one "Old Nell," who bought mostly whiskey in small amounts.

It is possible, by looking at the dates and amounts of weaving done by McCormick in 1776, to guess at the amount of clothing which was suddenly being made in the community, and to assume that much of it was to provide uniforms for those who had joined the regiment. (Although the accounts do not mention weaving assistants, it seems likely that McCormick would have had help in weaving such great lengths of fabric over short periods of time. McCormick had inherited several slaves when his father died.)

By May of 1778, William Crawford had been ordered by his superiors in the Continental Army to return to the Pennsylvania frontier to command the forces defending that front against Indians allied with the British.[32] In this effort he was joined by his son-in-law Harrison, and probably by others who had served with him in the 7th Virginia. Again a re-outfitting of the troops was demanded, and again this outfitting is reflected in William McCormick's account book.

Throughout the war McCormick continued to weave and to stay fairly close to home, as his accounts indicate. He was a member of the local militia during part of this time, charged with the safety of the

Table 1. McCormick's Weaving Accounts for 1776

Date	Fabric Type	Yardage	Per yard	Purchaser
Feb. 10	linen	35 yards	7 pence	William Crawford
Feb. 20	linen	21 yards	6 pence	Ann Connell
April 2	linen	7 yards	6 pence	William Harrison
April 20	linsey	12 yards	6 @10 pence	
			4 @9 pence	
			2 @8 pence	William Harrison
April 26	linen	26 yards	7 pence	Widow Harrison
May 3	linsey	12 yards	6 @10 pence	
			6 @8 pence	William Crawford
May 9	hemp	25 yards	7 pence	Ann Connell
May 20	hemp linen	49 yards	7 pence	James Egnew
May 22	linen	17 1/2 yards	8 pence	John Vance
June 8	linen	24 yards	7 pence	Robert Morreson
June 14	linen	19 yards	7 pence	William Harrison
June 20	linen	18 yards	15 @7 pence	
		3 striped	@3 shillings,	
			1 pence	Widow Harrison
June 27	linen	13 3/4 yards	8 @8 pence	
			3 1/2 @9 pence	
			1 1/2 @10 pence	John Crawford
July 2	linen	25 yards	7 pence	William Crawford
July 8	linen	17 yards	7 pence	William Skooler
July 20	linen	15 yards	6 pence	John Minton
Aug. 20	linen & linsey	13 yards	6 @ 9 pence	
			7 @ 7 pence	Paterick Larkin
Sept. 5	linen	10 yards	7 pence	William Harrison
Sept. 5	linen	19 yards	7 pence	William Crawford
Nov. 8	linen	4 yards	10 pence	John Crawford
Dec. 6	linen	37 yards	1 shilling	William Crawford

community.[33] In 1777 his accounts indicate that he wove abut 150 yards of fabric, down considerably from the year before. His account with David Linsey indicates clearly this account was for domestic linen, not for war supplies, stating charges for "weaving 15 yards of Lincy for Bety," and later, "weaving 15 yards of Lincy for your wife." He also supplied to William Makey, a member of his militia outfit, two dozen needles and three thimbles, and made shoes for several neighbors. He pastured a horse for his cousin Oliver, lending him a mare in replacement and charging Oliver for both. In addition to farming, raising hogs, horses, and sheep, and weaving, William and Effie also raised eleven children (although one died in infancy). In June of 1778, shortly after her father arrived to take command of the western forces, Effie had her fourth child in as many years (see figure 8).

In 1778 McCormick's accounts show his yardages to total about one hundred yards, but in 1779 this total fell to just thirteen yards, most of it during the first two months of the year. In that year it is likely that McCormick was a member of George Rogers Clark's Illinois campaign; Clark recruited many of his men, including a William McCormick, from among Virginians in western Pennsylvania.[34] The campaign to capture British outposts in Illinois was successful and McCormick returned to his home on the Youghioheny, probably by mid-September (another child was born to Effie in mid-June of 1780) and by 1780 was weaving again, although still not in very large quantities. After 1780 the accounts in the book are very scanty, and most entries are for William's private and generally scattered expenses.

In 1782 the McCormicks and the entire community were devastated by the shattering defeat of a large party of local men at the hands of Indians in Ohio, and by the deaths in that campaign of William Crawford, his son John, his son-in-law William Harrison, his nephew William Crawford, and many others. Colonel Crawford died after days of exquisite torture by the Indians, and graphic descriptions of his death inflamed the American frontier and entered into frontier literature.[35]

William McCormick continued to live in the same place in Pennsylvania for the next thirty-five years, owning a great deal of property and engaging in various kinds of business. The few biographical sketches which have been written about him say that in the 1790s he owned a saw mill on the banks of the Youghioheny near his home, in what is now a part of the corporate limits of Connellsville. The biographical accounts, borrowing as they do from each other, all mention that he was a trader or teamster, but none include his years as a weaver, a craft he apparently regarded as a practical necessity only during brief periods of his life.

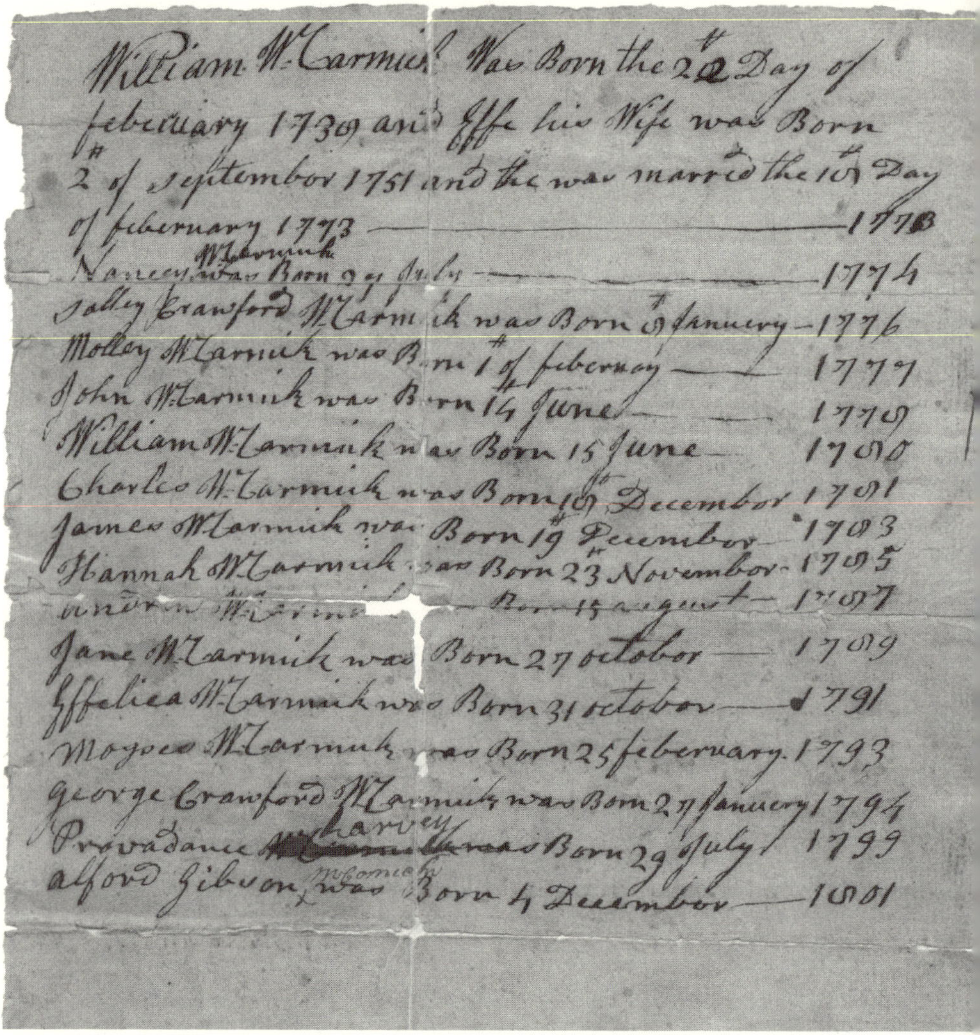

William McCarmick Was Born the 22 Day of
febeuary 1739 and Effe his Wife was Born
2 of september 1751 and the was marred the 10 Day
of feberuary 1773 —— 1773
Nancey McCormick was Born 9 of July —— 1774
sally Crawford McCarmick was Born 3 Januery — 1776
Molley McCarmick was Born 1 of feberuay — 1777
John McCarmick was Born 14 June — 1779
William McCarmick was Born 15 June — 1780
Charles McCarmick was Born 10 December 1781
James McCarmick was Born 19 December — 1783
Hannah McCarmick was Born 23 November — 1785
andrew Mc[illegible] [illegible] Born 18 august — 1787
Jane McCarmick was Born 27 october — 1789
Effelica McCarmick was Born 31 october — 1791
Moyses McCarmick was Born 25 feberuary 1793
george Crawford McCarmick was Born 27 Januery 1794
Provadance Harvey was Born 29 July 1799
alford Gibson McCormick was Born 4 December — 1801

Figure 8. This family record was written by William McCormick sometime after 1801; the paper was folded into the account book. On it he lists his birthdate and that of Effie Crawford, and the date of their marriage. Then he lists his children in order (the name obliterated by the horizontal fold is Andrew, born 18 August 1787). Eleven of those entries are their children, of whom one died in infancy; another was retarded. The last four entries are the children of Sarah (Sally) McCormick, who married John McCormick, a cousin. William lists one child as Provadance Harvey, but apparently his given name was Provance.

William McCormick was one of thousands of virtually trackless people who lived in America prior to the Revolution and in the early years of the republic, when it was possible to live without being officially recorded. Births were kept in family Bibles; marriages might not be recorded except in the record books of traveling ministers; taxes, especially from the western reaches of the territory, were imperfectly collected and noted; colonial censuses were irregular and incomplete; deaths were frequently unmarked except in private ways. McCormick seems to have managed a full, varied, and productive life in a pivotal time in America's history without being concerned about recording his participation. The few documents connected with him, such as his personal account book, allow an outline reconstruction of his adult life, and especially a reconstruction of the kind of cooperative commerce in which he participated on the Pennsylvania/Virginia frontier during years around the American Revolution.

Notes and References

1. It is possible to take a blind fragment of history and to identify it through a variety of sources, using it as a touchstone for revealing the social fabric of a community. My introduction to the world of William McCormick was casual: a friend showed me the account book as a curiosity. Curiosity has a way of escalating; from knowing only that the volume appeared to be an account book in English, dating from about the time of the American Revolution, I have come to know a great deal about who and what William McCormick was, and to conjecture a great deal more. Surnames were plentiful in the book; place names were not. By comparing the surnames to census indices and other sources, I now also know some of the "where" of William McCormick. In the fascinating process of reconstruction of his time, I have learned something of American history and much of the cooperative way of life on the frontier. Some of what I discovered follows in this paper. Positive microfilm copies of William McCormick's account book are housed at the Indiana Historical Society, Indianapolis, the Connellsville (PA) Public Library, and at the Kokomo-Howard County Public Library, Kokomo, IN.

2. John B. Linn and William H. Egle, eds., *Pennsylvania Archives,* Second Series, 3 (Harrisburg: State Printer of Pennsylvania, 1896), 552. Rolla Tryon, in *Household Manufactures in the United States, 1640–1860* (Chicago: University of Chicago Press, 1917), 112–13, said, "Long before the actual cutting off of this supply [of English goods] the family textile manufactures had come to be a positive factor in the common life and prosperity of the ... middle colonies.... In the absence of adequate textile manufacturing establishments, the homes were the main reliance for this

type of goods." Stevenson W. Fletcher, in *Pennsylvania Agriculture and Country Life* (Harrisburg: Pennsylvania Historical and Museum Commission, 1950), 423, suggested that women bartered home manufactured linen goods and that "spinning was the almost universal employment of farm women."

3. See William R. Bagnall, *The Textile Industries of the United States*, vol. I (Cambridge: Riverside Press, 1893), 50; Elizabeth and Solon Buck, *The Planting of Civilization in Western Pennsylvania* (Pittsburgh: University of Pittsburgh Press, 1939), 309; and Fletcher, *Pennsylvania Agriculture*, 423. Buck and Fletcher both reported that "on January 21, 1797, the *Pittsburgh Gazette* printed an item from Philadelphia announcing the establishment in that city of a 'most curious and extensively useful Manufactory, in which the spinning and weaving of hemp, flax, and tow are performed by means of machinery. . . .'" In 1753 in Connecticut, a John Bulkley of Colchester had petitioned unsuccessfully to set up a monopolistic business dressing flax, using water-driven machines "similar to the machines recently invented and set up in Scotland." A few months later, according to Bagnall, two successful petitioners were given a fifteen-year monopoly to do the same.

4. Many authors have commented on the use of barter and trade systems rather than currency. Fletcher, in *Pennsylvania Agriculture*, 289, quoted an informed source as saying, "the words *buy* and *sell* are unknown here [on the western Pennsylvania frontier]; in business nothing is heard but the word *trade*." See also his discussion of storekeeping and neighbors' accounts, 276, and George Dallas Albert, *History of Westmoreland County, Pennsylvania* (Philadelphia: L. H. Everts, 1882), 160, on the practice of paying neighborhood linen weavers in yard goods, as well as Joseph Doddridge, *Notes on the Settlement and Indian Wars of the Western Parts of Virginia and Pennsylvania* (1st edition, 1824; revised edition, Akron, OH: The New Werner Co., 1912), 113–14.

5. Some examples of eighteenth-century linen-faced quilts, tops and bed covers are: "Octagon Appliqué" top, MA or NH, 1782–1800 (28–29) and "Tide Mill," Mary Dingee Priestley, Ossining, NY, 1785–1810 (30–31), in *Quilts from the Shelburne Museum* (Tokyo: Kokusai Art, 1996). See also "Eliza Armstead Miller Quilt," VA, late eighteenth century (Plate 38), 121, all white counterpane, Mrs. Thaddeus Burr, Fairfield, CT, second half of the eighteenth century (Figure 84), 184, "Framed Center Quilt," maker unknown, probably MA, c. 1800 (Plate 40), 124, and crewel-embroidered quilt with pieced border, maker unknown, CT, second half of the eighteenth century (Plate 41), 125, in Myron and Patsy Orlofsky, *Quilts in America* (NY: McGraw Hill Book Co., 1974). See also "Whole Cloth," Eve Van Cortlandt, Bronx Co., NY, 1760 (Figure 8), 8, and Tambour quilt, Mildred—, Cos Cob, Rye, NY, 1753 (Figure 11), 10, in Jacqueline M. Adkins and Phyllis Tepper, *New York Beauties, Quilts from the Empire State* (NY: Dutton Studio Books, 1992). Many sources do not list the fiber content of illustrated quilts in the collections.

6. For information on the production of linen cloth see John Wiley, *A Treatise on the Propagation of Sheep, the Manufacture of Wool, and the Cultivation and Manufacture of Flax* (Williamsburg: F. Royle, 1765); Frances Little, *Early American Textiles* (New York: The Century Co., 1931); *All Sorts of Good Sufficient Cloth: Linen Making*

in New England 1640–1860 (North Andover, MA: Merrimack Valley Textile Museum, 1980); Nancy Dick Bogdonoff, *Handwoven Textiles of Early New England* (Harrisburg, PA: Stackpole Books, 1975); and Sandra Rambo Walker, *Country Cloth to Coverlets, Textile Traditions in 19th Century Central Pennsylvania* (Lewisburg, PA: Oral Traditions Project of the Union County Historical Society, 1981).

7. See, for instance, numerous entries in Junie E. S. King, *Abstracts of Wills, Inventories, and Administrations Accounts of Frederick County, Virginia* (Scottsdale, AZ: n.p., 1961), for examples of wills in which articles of clothing were left to specific recipients. The practice was common throughout the eighteenth century. Early nineteenth century wills recorded in frontier areas reflect the same practice.

8. In 1755 troops under General Edward Braddock, Commander in Chief of British forces in America, attempted to cut a road through the wilderness of Pennsylvania to attack the French at Ft. Duquesne (Pittsburgh). They were surprised and ambushed by the French and Indians on July 9 near present-day Uniontown, and over half the force was killed. Braddock was among the casualties; one of his staff, George Washington, was responsible for leading the survivors to safety. Nearly twenty years later the Rev. David McClure passed through the area and wrote in his diary that to the disgrace of the current British command, the bones of the dead were still scattered on the ground, ravaged by animals and showing marks of the scalping knife. Cited in John Harpster, ed., "The Diary of David McClure," *Pen Pictures of Early Western Pennsylvania* (Pittsburgh: University of Pittsburgh Press, 1938), 120.

9. Tryon, *Household Manufactures*, 108–110; Fletcher, *Pennsylvania Agriculture*, 284; Theodore Thayer, *Pennsylvania Politics and the Growth of Democracy, 1740–1776* (Harrisburg: Pennsylvania Historical and Museum Commission, 1953), 144; and Bagnall, *Textile Industries*, 55.

10. Bagnall, Ibid., 53.

11. Ibid., 55; Tryon, *Household Manufactures*, 54–55, reports that in 1769 the seniors at Brown University also graduated wearing domestic fabrics.

12. Tryon, Ibid., 54, from the *Pennsylvania Journal* of 20 April 1769, as cited in newspaper extracts from the *New Jersey Archives*, 1st Series, XXVI.

13. Ibid., 55, from the *New York Journal* of 30 May 1768, as cited in Paterson, *History of Rhode Island*, 111.

14. Carl Bridenbaugh, *The Colonial Craftsman* (New York: New York University Press, 1950), 35, quotes Samuel Powel in 1743.

15. The legal history of the original Shenandoah grants is a complicated one that has been historically controversial. James G. Leyburn, in *The Scotch-Irish: A Social History* (Chapel Hill: University of North Carolina Press, 1967), attributed the major grants to Fairfax and Beverley; Thomas K. Cartmell, in the earlier *Shenandoah Valley Pioneers and their Descendants* (Winchester, VA., n.p., 1909), said John Van Meter was the original purchaser, and that Joist Hite purchased from him. That the grants were in contention is well-documented; a lengthy suit between Fairfax and Hite, which Fairfax lost, resolved ownership for those who had purchased from Hite.

16. John W. Jordan, ed., *Genealogical and Personal History of Fayette County, Penn-*

sylvania, III (New York: Lewis Historical Publishing Co., 1912), 368. Jordan says "The White House" was built in 1740 and was still standing in 1903.

17. *Colonial and Revolutionary Lineages of America*, vol. X (New York: American History Company, Inc., 1943), 247–51.

18. King, *Abstracts of Wills*, 13.

19. A good general reference is Alfred H. Shorter, *Paper Mills and Paper Makers in England 1495–1800* (Halversum, Holland: The Paper Publications Society, 1957). I am grateful to the librarians at the Lilly Rare Books Library, Indiana University, Bloomington, Indiana, for their assistance in determining that the watermark on the pages of McCormick's account book indicated that the paper was made by James Whatman. Whatman's paper mill in Kent made papers bearing that mark from 1750 to 1759. The source for this information is Shorter; see also Edward Heawood, *Watermarks, Mainly of the 17th and 18th Centuries* (Halversum, Holland: The Paper Publications Society, 1950).

20. Harpster, "Diary of David McClure," *Pen Pictures*, 8.

21. The political boundary between Pennsylvania and Virginia was in contention for years, necessitating a survey by Mason and Dixon to decide it. Those Virginians who moved into the "Yough" region south of Fort Pitt did so as citizens of their home colony, developing its western area. Until 1779, when Virginia finally gave up claim to the area, the region where McCormick teamstered and later lived was successively Augusta County, West Augusta, and Yohogania County, Virginia, *and simultaneously* Cumberland, Bedford, Westmoreland, and finally Fayette County, Pennsylvania. Each colony established jurisdictional offices for such things as courts, survey and land offices, and peace offices. William Crawford, who lived in the Yough and who was to be William McCormick's father-in-law, served as a justice of the peace for Pennsylvania but served Virginia in Lord Dunmore's War at the same time. See the following for some of the intricacies of the situation: James Veech, *The Monongahela of Old* (privately printed, 1858–92; reprinted Waynesburg, PA: Greene County Historical Society, 1971), 99; Buck, *Planting of Civilization*, 162; Consul W. Butterfield, *The Washington-Crawford Letters Concerning Western Lands (1767–1781)* (Cincinnati: Robert Clarke & Co., 1877), viii-ix. Wayland F. Dunaway, in *The Scotch Irish of Colonial Pennsylvania* (Chapel Hill: University of North Carolina Press, 1944), 75, said "prior to 1779, when Virginia yielded to Pennsylvania her claim to this territory, the majority of the settlers there were Virginians holding their lands under Virginia title.... the [Virginia] purchase price was only 2 shillings, 6 pence per hundred acres, whereas the Pennsylvania price was five pounds per hundred acres, besides one penny per acre quitrent."

22. Cited in *Centennial History of Connellsville*, 29–30, this text is from the original *Calendar of State Papers of Virginia*, 280–82: "Colonel William Crawford, Deposeth and saith, that his first acquaintance with the Country on the Ohio was in the year 1758, he then being an officer in the Virginia Service — That between that time and the year 1765, a number of Settlements were made on the Public Roads in that Country by Permission of the Several Commanding Officers at Fort Pitt. That in the Fall of the Year 1765 he made some Improvements on the West Side of

the Alleghany [sic] Mountains, in the Spring of the year following he setled [sic] and has continued to live out here ever since. —That, before that time, and in that year, a Considerable number of Settlements were made, he thinks near three hundred, without Permission from any Commanding Officer, some of which settlements were made within the Limits of the Indiania Company's Claim, and some others within Col. Croghan's."

23. Buck, in *Planting of Civilization*, 231, reported that Baltimore, Frederick, Hagerstown, Oldtown, and Cumberland were Southern stops; Thayer (*Pennsylvania Politics*, 129) said that Susquehanna trade with Baltimore made it a serious rival to Philadelphia for frontier produce. Maryland encouraged this trade by road improvements. See Albert, *History of Westmoreland County*, 180–81, and Veech, *Monongahela of Old*, 37–38, for detailed descriptions of the pack-horse trade. In Historical Committee of the Connellsville Centennial Celebration, eds., *Centennial History of Connellsville* (Columbus, OH: Champlin Press, 1906), 38, McCormick is described as a professional packer. No source mentions his trade as a weaver of linen goods.

24. Pennsylvania continued to pay a bounty on scalps until 1782, when graphic accounts of the savagery of William Crawford's death shocked populace and government alike. See C. Hale Sipe, *The Indian Wars of Pennsylvania* (Harrisburg: The Telegraph Press, 1929), 625, as cited in *Pennsylvania Archives*, First Series, 8: 167, 176, 283, 369, 393.

25. Genealogical and historical sources all agree that William McCormick came to the present-day site of Connellsville about 1770, and that he lived across the river from the Crawfords. See Franklin Ellis, ed., *History of Fayette County, Pennsylvania* (Philadelphia: L.H. Everts & Co., 1882), 355, and Jordon, *Fayette County*, 368. In 1889 John M. Gresham, ed., *Biographical and Portrait Cyclopedia of Fayette County, Pennsylvania* (Chicago: John M. Gresham & Co., 1889), 450, reported that William and Effie McCormick's log house still stood, "the oldest house in the town of Connellsville." But Ellis described (355) two other McCormick homesteads, one "below the stone house on the Davidson farm," and another "large log house where is now the stone house built by John Boyd." Ellis's book appears to be a vanity book, and is otherwise flawed; he may also be mistaken about these structures.

26. Harpster, "Diary of David McClure," *Pen Pictures*, 122–23. I have found no record of William and Effie's marriage except the one William left in his book. It is likely that they were married by a circuit-riding preacher, and that the record remains with his papers.

27. In 1766, 70,000 bushels of flaxseed were shipped from Philadelphia to Europe, most of it Pennsylvania-grown and bound for Ireland and England (Fletcher, *Pennsylvania Agriculture*, 162). But in the next year, a rumor that flax was banned for export made it nearly worthless (Thayer, *Pennsylvania Politics*, 144). By 1771 the market had reached its peak; that year Pennsylvania exported 110,000 bushels (Fletcher, *Pennsylvania Agriculture*, 282). In 1774 there was a general failure of the flax crop. See Anne Bezanson, *Prices and Inflation during the American Revolution; Pennsylvania, 1770–1790* (Philadelphia: University of Pennsylvania Press, 1951),

289, note. By 1775 embargoes and home use had caused a significant drop in all exports, including flaxseed.

28. Doddridge reported that only three whites were killed by Indians in Fayette County during frontier days, saying "Fayette, like some sections of Washington County, was practically immune from savage forays" (Doddridge, *Notes*, 312). But in a letter to George Washington on June 8, 1774, William Crawford reported that he had found it necessary to build a fort near his house, and so had his brother Valentine (Butterfield, *Washington-Crawford Letters*). Despite the absence of fatalities, alarms were frequent enough to keep people away from their homes and "forted up" for safety.

29. Linn and Egle, *Pennsylvania Archives*, Second Series, 3: 551–54. William McCormick, although he benefited by his labor, does not seem to have violated this edict. The cooperative labor system would have precluded profit-taking, since each man valued his own labor and skills, but was dependent upon agreement of that value for the successful conclusion of business. Throughout McCormick's accounts, weaving costs for linen hover around seven pence per yard. Bezanson gives figures for the cost of fabric during the boycott years and the cost after 1776, but does not specifically mention labor costs (Bezanson, *Prices and Inflation*, 285, 291).

30. The continental forces were plagued throughout the war by supply problems, including a supply of proper clothing. *Pennsylvania Archives* is full of requests for clothing supplies, citing the poor quality of previous goods, the weather, the ever-present problem of desertion, and the confusion of responsibility for provision of clothing as reasons. December 23, 1777, various officers petitioned the Pennsylvania Executive Council for immediate action on their needs, saying: "we have apply'd to the Cloathier Gen'l, and are Informed he Cannot supply our demands without Injureing the rest of the army, and not even then. A Recent Resolve of Congress, published Lately in Gen'l Orders, recommends to the Legislatures of the sev'l United States to provide Cloathing for their respective quotas of Troops" (*Pennsylvania Archives*, Second Series, 3: 130). By 1778 the requests urged the Council's awareness of "the miserable and alarming Situation of the Pennsylvania Troop for want of necessary Cloathing. . . . Our Men have been without a Rag of Linen on their Backs, for Weeks, nay months at a Time, [and] our applications to the Cloathier General's Store, have proved fruitless" (*Pennsylvania Archives*, Second Series, 3: 174–75).

31. Gresham, *Fayette County*, 450. Charles Hannah, in *The Wilderness Trail* (New York: G.P. Putnam's Sons, 1911), 79–80, reported that in 1775 the names of Crawford and Harrison, along with Valentine Crawford and John Stephenson (Crawford's brother and half-brother), had been sent to the British government as "Persons Well-disposed to His Majesty's Government, Living on the Frontiers of Virginia . . . At the Allegheny Mountains, and to be heard of at Ft. Pitt." The following year Crawford became a Lieutenant Colonel in the 5th Virginia Regiment, and then commanded the 7th. Next, according to Butterfield (*Washington-Crawford Letters*, x), he raised the 13th, a West Augusta regiment to be raised west of the Alleghenies: "In August of 1777, with about 200 of his new levies, Craw-

ford joined the main army under Washington, who was then near Philadelphia." Harrison was also a colonel, commanding an artillery regiment. Responding to a letter of August 9, 1777, from Governor Patrick Henry of Virginia, Congress settled the matter of allegiance: "any officer now in Col. Harrison's regiment of artillery shall have liberty to leave the said regiment on being appointed to any office or command in the corps of artillery raising or to be raised in Virginia by the said State (*Pennsylvania Archives*, Second Series, 3: 104). These conflicts and apparent contradictions were the result of continuing jurisdictional disputes over the western frontier by Virginia and Pennsylvania.

32. Gresham, *Fayette County*, 450; Francis B. Heitman, *Historical Register of Officers of the Continental Army* (Washington: Rare Book Shop Publishing Co., 1914), 177; Butterfield, *Washington-Crawford Letters*, x; and Sipe, *Indian Wars*, 573, 568–70. In 1778 Crawford built Ft. Crawford, on the east bank of the Allegheny River in Westmoreland County, at the site of present-day Parnassus, PA. In September of that year he attended a treaty at Fort Pitt with his brother John Stephenson, at which the Delawares agreed to ally themselves with the Americans in exchange for a promise of gaining a sovereign state in the union at the successful conclusion of the conflict (from Sipe).

33. Richard Loveless, *Records of the District of West Augusta, Ohio County, and Yohogania County, Virginia* (Columbus, OH: Ohio State University Printing Department, 1970), 139, 240; McCormick was made a lieutenant in the militia in 1778, taking the oath of office and (411) was made a captain in 1780.

34. John H. Gwathmey, *Historical Register of Virginians in the Revolution* (Baltimore: Genealogical Publishing Co., 1979), cites Illinois State Papers for William McCormick in Clark's Illinois Regiment.

35. For a contemporary account of the affair see Baron Rosenthal ("John Rose"), *Journal of a Volunteer Expedition to Sandusky from May 24 to June 13, 1782* (New York: New York Times and Arno Press, 1969), and Consul W. Butterfield, *Historical Account of the Expedition Against Sandusky under Col. William Crawford in 1782* (Cincinnati: Robert Clarke, 1873). Butterfield's account is later but based on oral and eyewitness accounts.

✳ ✳ ✳

Creating a New Tradition: Quilting in Tonga

Phyllis S. Herda

The western Polynesian islands of Tonga have a long tradition of textiles (barkcloth and fine plaited mats) being valued as items of significance and wealth. Recently Tongan women have expanded this textile repertoire to include machine-made quilts and an identifiable Tongan style of quilts is emerging. Tongan quilts are now a prominent feature of grave decorations. In addition, they are displayed and presented at a wide variety of functions including births, weddings, anniversaries, title installations, and royal celebrations. The introduction of and acceptance of quilts to this repertoire is inextricably linked to establishment of Tongan migrant communities overseas—especially in the United States. This paper examines Tongan quilts, the social and political occasions in which they are ritualized as well as the diasporic effects on quiltmaking and on the display and presentation of quilts.

Sewing, piecing and appliquéing quilts is a relatively new textile tradition in the islands of Tonga. The creation, display, and presentation of traditional textiles, mats woven from pandanus leaves (*kie, ngafingafi* or *fala*) and cloth made from the bark of the paper mulberry tree (*ngatu* or *tapa*), however, has an ancient and distinguished history in the islands.[1] Tongans have long categorized these textiles, all made by women, as wealth or *koloa*—"what one values" and have accorded them the highest respect in terms of the protocols of exchange. In comparison, the work, carving and agricultural, of men, *ngaue*, is best translated simply as work or labor. Textile wealth made by Tongan women reflects their high status and rank in comparison to their brothers. When it is presented, women's textile wealth also actively demonstrates status differences between chiefly (*'eiki*) and non-chiefly (*tu'a*) individuals. The creation of these traditional textiles continues today, much in the same way as it has for centuries; however, Tongan women have also expanded their textile repertoire to include quilts in order to fulfill cultural expectations at significant life events including births, first birthdays, weddings, anniversary celebrations, title installations and, most commonly, at funerals or as grave decorations.

This innovation, while on the one hand representing a departure from past practices, has also served to complement rather than replace traditional Tongan practices involving textile wealth. Indeed, it is clear that women's critical role in producing textile wealth has remained central to social and economic exchange in Tonga, although in some cases the parameters of these exchanges have shifted. Cloth has remained central to the organization of social as well as political life for Tongans. The quilts, as a form of textile wealth, provide a connection between the home islands and Tongans who have migrated overseas, mostly to the United States, and a means of connecting with a Tongan identity in a traditionally based manner while also creatively claiming a unique migrant identity. This paper examines Tongan quilting and how it fits into the larger Tongan textile tradition.

The Kingdom of Tonga

The islands of Tonga are part of western Polynesia, lying just east of Fiji and south of Samoa between 15° S. and 24° S. latitudes and between 173° W. and 175° W. longitudes (see figure 1). Anthropologists and archaeologists designate this region as nuclear Polynesia where over three thousand years ago people, almost assuredly from the west, settled in the area and established a cultural complex which is now known as Polynesian.[2] It seems clear that cloth was an important item in this cultural system from its earliest days.[3] From the Tongan and probably Samoan islands, intrepid Polynesian sailors and explorers set out and settled the far eastern reaches of the region—Tahiti and the Society Islands, the Marquesas, the Hawaiian Islands, Aotearoa/New Zealand, the Cook Islands, and Rapanui/Easter Island as well as many other smaller archipelagoes and islands.[4]

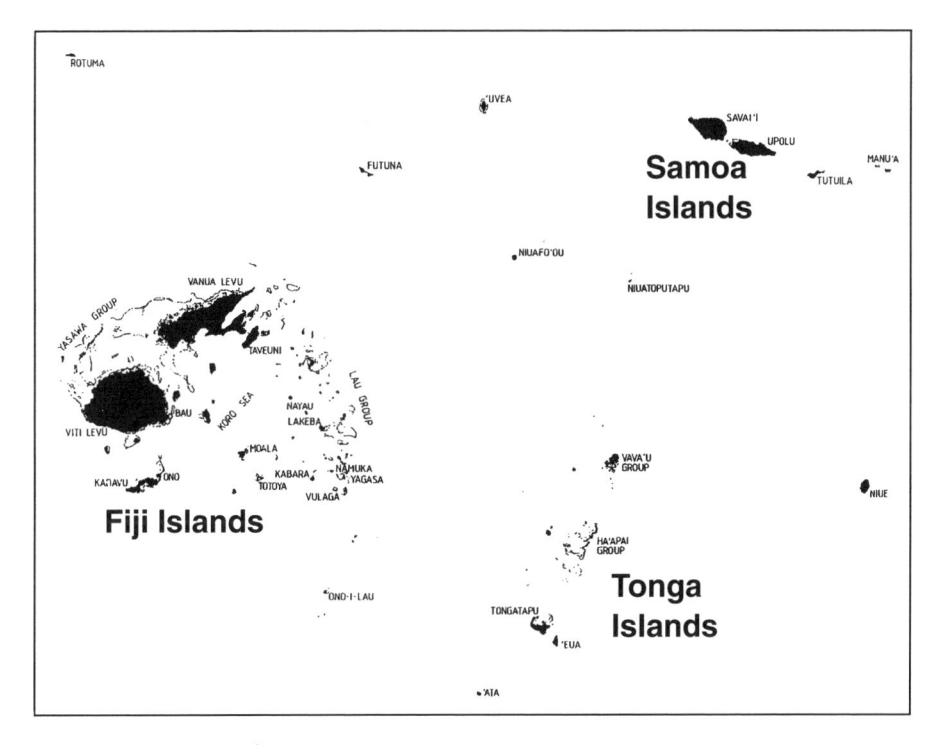

Figure 1. Western Polynesia

Over 150 islands and islets, stretched over several hundred kilometers of ocean, make up the Tongan archipelago. Historically, Tongans were renowned sailors and they have always maintained ongoing kin, social, and political ties within the archipelago as well as beyond their shores, particularly with the Samoan Islands and the Lau Islands of Fiji.[5] Tonga, both traditionally and contemporarily, is a hierarchical society with a complex ranking system based on gender and birth. It is often described as one of the mostly highly stratified and centralized of the Polynesian societies.[6] Those who are deemed "chiefly" (*'eiki*) rule—traditionally in a somewhat fluid combination of sacred and ruling titled chiefs. Since 1845 that rule has been a constitutional monarchy self-proclaimed by Taufa'ahau Tupou I who, in an effort to repulse imperialistic Europeans, promulgated codes of law and, eventually, a constitution, in a western style. He also established a royal dynasty which still survives and rules Tonga today.

Tongan contact with the West began with the very brief call of a Dutch expedition in 1643, but remained fleeting and sporadic until the visits of James Cook and his crew in the 1770s. Contact with the West was intermittent in the 1780s and 1790s, but from the turn of the nineteenth century it has remained almost continuous.[7] Christian missionaries arrived on the islands in 1797, with a permanent Wesleyan presence established in the mid 1820s, with other Christian sects and orders arriving after this.[8] Today, Christianity, as expressed by a wide variety of denominations, plays a very important part in Tongan life and culture—both in the islands and in migrant communities overseas.

Emmigration from Tonga to the West, primarily to the United States, Aotearoa/New Zealand, and Australia, began in the late 1950s with significant increases in the 1960s and 1970s as western economies burgeoned and factory work was readily available for migrant workers.[9] It is difficult to overestimate the impact that this migration has had on Tonga—a small kingdom with a population of about 100,000. Virtually every Tongan family has some of its members living, temporarily or permanently, overseas and, at times, remittances from overseas have proved economically significant for many families. It has been estimated that by the twenty-first century more Tongans will live outside of the Kingdom, than inside its boundaries.[10] Most of these emigrants, however, keep close ties with family in the Islands, returning regularly for visits to the Islands when they are able and participating, even if from afar, in the significant life events of family members. Quilts have come to play an important part in fulfilling kin obligations through their presentation both in home islands and between home and overseas migrant communities of Tongan people.

The Introduction of Quilting in Tonga

Tongan women have been crocheting, piecing, and quilting to produce utilitarian bedcovers for quite some time. There is some debate as to where women learned the craft and when they began quilting. It is generally agreed that quilt making was prevalent in the years following the Second World War and, most probably, that it existed to a lesser extent before the War. It is not so clear, however, where and from whom Tongan women learned to quilt. Some Tongans contend that they were taught by Christian missionaries (American Mormon missionaries, the wives of British Wesleyan missionaries, or Catholic sisters are all mentioned as possibilities). Others credit the Peace Corps workers from the United States with their introduction. Still others believe that Tongan women learned while living overseas—the United States is most frequently mentioned as the source.

In truth, the introduction of quilting in Tonga has probably come from several sources at different times in history. The most likely of the missionary sources is the Mormon church. A permanent Mormon mission was established in Tonga in 1916 and, presumably, the female missionaries brought their quilting skills with them and taught local women as they did elsewhere in the Pacific.[11] This is certainly supported by the generic name, "*Kuilti Mamonga*" ("Mormon quilts"), applied by some Tongans to the craft. It need not, however, be the sole source. Wesleyan wives accompanied their missionary husbands into the Tongan mission fields since the 1820s. Sewing was a skill they eagerly taught and it was equally eagerly learned.[12] There is also clear evidence that individual female Peace Corps workers, resident in the islands since the 1960s, who were also quilters, taught Tongan women their skills. Other western women who lived in the islands also influenced quilting. An Australian and New Zealand woman, for example, helped establish a quilting co-operative in the 1980s which made bed covers and cot quilts for sale. Many Tongan women living overseas, especially in Hawai'i and the Mainland U.S.A., took up quilting, and brought it back to the Kingdom during visits or when they returned to live. In addition, the local commerical bookstore regularly imports quilt books and magazines. Undoubtedly all of these sources played a role in the establishment of quilting in Tonga.

Annette B. Weiner and Jane Schneider argue that humans imbue cloth with symbolic potentials for social cohesion and political salience and that these are manifest in at least four domains of social activity.[13] The first is in the creation of the cloth itself and how this is perceived. The second involves human rituals surrounding and signifying life events, especially death. The third domain is in the rituals surrounding ceremonial investitures of power and authority. Clothing and personal adornment and decoration comprises the fourth domain. In contemporary Tonga it is possible to trace the culturally significant embodiment of quilts in the existing textile tradition by their inclusion in the first three domains as identified by Weiner and Schneider.

Quilts as Grave Decoration and Funerary Gifts

The first area in which quilts appeared as more than bed linen was as grave decoration or art and as funerary gifts. As Weiner notes, women and cloth, by providing a means of descent group regeneration, play a significant part in rituals surrounding death in Polynesia.[14] Grave decoration is regarded as a significant and culturally valued female art from in Tonga. By decorating and caring for the grave, Tongan women show their love *('ofa)* and respect *(fak'apa'apa)* for their deceased relation. The decoration can take on a variety of forms including the creation of a border by the placement of stones, the building of cement footings or low walls, or the careful upside down burying of beer or other bottles. Within these borders and over the entire grave, mounds of white sand or crushed coral are piled to glisten in the tropical sun. Small, black stones which have been specially oiled for the purpose, flowers, shells or other decorations are placed in and on the sand and coral. In addition, a *tapu*, a banner-like piece of cloth attached to a structure, usually made of wood, to hold it taut and upright, is erected at the head of the grave.[15] *Tapu* signifies something sacred or forbidden in Tongan and it is this sentiment with which Tongans regard graves and cemeteries and why the placement of *tapu* is important. The inclusion of textiles at the head of the grave as a *tapu* is a traditional practice in Tonga and reflects respect, as textiles are the quintessential form of Tongan wealth, to the deceased. Traditionally, mats, barkcloth, or "skirts" *(sisi)* made of sweet smelling flowers *(tapu kakala)* were used in their construction; however, since the 1970s quilts have been employed as grave *tapu* and as funerary gifts to appropriate family members.[16]

Initially, these *tapu* quilts were made by Tongan women living overseas, mostly in the United States, who found themselves unable to fulfill normal funerary expectations when a close relative died. Living away from the islands, in an environment where the raw materials for traditional *tapu* were unavailable and often unable, usually due to financial constraints, to make the trip back to Tonga for the funeral, these migrant women created textile *tapu* by working with cloth and creating quilts.

The first quilt *tapu* were almost all pieced, patchwork quilts in traditional western star patterns, such as Blazing Star, Eight-Pointed Star, Pieced Star, Virginia Star, and, especially, the pattern often identified as the Lone Star or Morning Star. The Lone Star/Morning Star designs which feature one large star depicted across the entire quilt surface, pieced from many, small, diamond-shaped pieces, remains an enduring favorite in Tongan *tapu* quilts (see figure 2). Star design patchworks, in general, are popular for *tapu* quilts (see figure 3). The majority of the Kingdom's citizens are Christian, many devoutly so, and the biblical association of star quilts undoubtedly adds to their appeal

Figure 2. Lone Star/Morning Star patchwork quilt as grave *tapu*; Tongatapu, Kingdom of Tonga, 1999. Photograph by the author.

Figure 3. Star patchwork quilts as grave *tapu*; Tongatapu, Kingdom of Tonga, 1998. Photograph by the author.

and inclusion as *tapu*. Other traditional patchwork designs used by Tongan quilters include: Bear's Paw, Drunkard's Path, Grandmother's Flower Garden, Mariner's Compass, Monkey Wrench, and Weathervane; although it should be noted that Tongan women rarely know or use the names of the Western patterns. An interesting twist on Tongan textiles was the inclusion of a traditional Western patchwork pattern, Grandmother's Fan on a piece of recently made Tongan barkcloth (see figure 4). In the early 1990s, puff quilts, where pieced squares are individually stuffed with a fluffy batting, became very popular as *tapu* and quilts for commemorative rituals, as the name of the deceased could be easily and distinctively spelled out with the squares making a lovely memorial piece (see figure 5).

Appliquéd designs that are executed in a Hawaiian-style appliqué, are now common in Tongan *tapu* quilts. The "Hawaiian style" is a symmetrical design achieved by folding the cloth into fourths or, sometimes, eighths before cutting layers. The overall effect is of a paper-cut snowflake. Rather than one design across the entire quilt, as is common in Hawaiian appliqué, Tongans prefer to repeat the designs in an album style (see figure 6). Tongan, unlike Hawaiian, quilts are almost

Quilting in Tonga

Figure 4. Patchwork design known as Grandmother's Fan used as a design on a piece of barkcloth (*ngatu*); Nuku'alofa, Kingdom of Tonga, 1999. Photograph by the author.

Figure 5. Puff quilt grave *tapu* spelling out name of the deceased; Tongatapu, Kingdom of Tonga, 1999. Photograph by the author.

Figure 6. Hawaiian-style album appliqué grave *tapu*; Tongatapu, Kingdom of Tonga, 1999. Photograph by the author.

always machine pieced, appliquéd, and quilted and do not follow the intricate quilting patterns evident in Hawaiian quilts.[17] Tongan innovation in appliquéd design can also be seen to be emerging in new and original asymmetrical designs.

Bright and colorful metallic fabrics are often utilized for *tapu* quilts as they add a shininess which is regarded as beautiful and pleasing in Tongan aesthetics (see figure 7). In this same vein, shiny Christmas ornaments, tinsel, or garland as well as swags of bright and ostentatious sequined, lame, velvet, or other fabric, usually reserved for night club wear in the West, are often strung up around the grave. Recently a string of electric Christmas lights was added to a grave in a cemetery in the suburbs of Nuku'alofa, the capital of Tonga. The lights gaily twinkled throughout the night. Non-Western color combinations of usually plain and always bright fabric or of white and one other color are becoming recognizable Tongan styles in *tapu* and other forms

Quilting in Tonga

Figure 7. Lone Star/Morning Star patchwork grave *tapu* pieced from favored metallic fabric; Tongatapu, Kingdom of Tonga, 1995. Photograph by the author.

of Tongan quilt design (see figures 8 and 9). The desire seems to be for bold, bright colors to catch the eye. The color and texture of the cloth is deemed aesthetically pleasing by Tongans and is in stark contrast to the black mourning clothes worn by relatives of the deceased.

Many of these *tapu* are, strictly speaking, bed coverlets, not quilts, because they are made of only two layers—the top design on the foundation backing, instead of several layers of cloth and batting which are sewn or quilted together. Colloquially the *tapu*, whether or not they are batted and quilted, are still called quilts. The *tapu* are left on the grave at the mercy of the weather, often until they literally fall down or fall apart (see figure 10). Even then, new *tapu* are often simply attached over the old frayed ones. This is done out of respect for the dead as well as the quiltmakers. Other women regularly refresh the *tapu* and the other grave decorations.

As with the creation of traditional Tongan textiles, the fact that the women process the cloth—in this case by cutting, piecing, stitching, and appliquéing it—thereby transforming it into something new, has

Figure 8. Pieced quilt in contrasting colors; Tongatapu, Kingdom of Tonga, 1999. Photograph by the author.

significance. Weiner and Schneider identify this as a pan-human trait with regards to cloth.[18] In pre-Christian, pre-monarchical Tonga, the making of barkcloth and the weaving of mats was an activity whereby the status, rank, and "essence" (*mana*) of the maker was transferred or imbued to the cloth in the creation process. In the communal barkcloth work groups this transfer and imbuing inevitably followed rank, with the cloth being "owned" by or, more accurately described as, being associated with the woman of chiefly rank who would have organized the work group. She controlled its production and its distribution.[19] Like the traditional textile processes, quiltmaking embodied the maker's status and, significantly, the maker's relationship to the deceased in a manner relevant to them—their *'ofa* (love) and *faka'apa'apa* (respect) was clear in the cloth they constructed, even if the cloth, itself, looked different. This is most likely the reason Tongan women living overseas preferred making quilts rather than purchasing traditional mats and barkcloth which, except for the finest mats, are readily

Quilting in Tonga

Figure 9. Pieced quilt in contrasting colors, presented to the owner by her brother; Nuku'alofa, Kingdom of Tonga, 1999. Photograph by the author.

Figure 10. Grave *tapu* deteriorating with age; Tongatapu, Kingdom of Tonga, 1999. Photograph by the author.

available for purchase at the market in Nuku'alofa or through private sales or commissions.

These first grave quilts were not well received in Tonga. Women and men I spoke with remembered being dismayed at the lack of sensibilities towards tradition with regards to this form of grave decoration. They were shocked when the quilts, along with lengths of manufactured cloth, began appearing as *tapu* on the graves themselves in the 1970s. Twenty-five years later, however, beautifully pieced and appliquéd quilts, sometimes made in Tonga, adorn graves throughout the Kingdom; although they are still most prevalent on Tonga *tapu*. Whereas six or seven quilts might have been present in large Tonga *tapu* cemeteries in the early 1990s when I began my research; up to thirty or forty were counted in large cemeteries in 1999.

Many, if not most, of the women who were formerly shocked and dismayed, now view the quilts as attractive, durable and, hence, practical grave decorations which are entirely appropriate in the Tongan setting. The quilts are most often made by mothers, sisters, or wives of the deceased and, in some cases, were made during the lifetime of the deceased. Their inclusion as *tapu* at the grave expresses the double meaning of quilt as a form of traditional textile wealth (*koloa*) and also as a form of bed linen in the everlasting sleep of the deceased. They are clearly part of an emerging textile aesthetic in Tongan grave art.[20]

The Ritual Presentation of Quilts

Titles, inherited through the male line, are an important part of Tongan politics. Although having a traditional basis, since the 1876 constitution a named Tongan nobility is based around male titleholders. Part of the ritual surrounding the installation of a new titleholder involves the pounding and hydration of *kava*, a drink made from the root of the plant which is often served in Tonga at important social and political events.[21] In a formal *kava* ceremony, the titles of all present are called out as their cup of *kava* is brought to them. During an installation ceremony, the title is bestowed when the new holder's title is called out for the first time. This is accompanied by a presentation of goods and valuables to the highest ranking chief in a ceremony

Quilting in Tonga

Figure 11. Investiture ceremony (*pongipongi hingoa*) for the Tu'i Lakepa titleholder. Palace Grounds, Kolomotu'a, Kingdom of Tonga, 1993. Photograph by the author.

known as *pongipongi hingoa*. Cloth, as the acknowledged highest form of wealth, has been presented at these investiture ceremonies as long as anyone can remember. In post-Constitutional Tonga, the "highest chief" is the monarch of the Kingdom of Tonga with the titleholder coming from the ranks of named nobility.

Quilts first made their way into the *pongipongi hingoa* in the 1993 installation of the "Tu'i Lakepa" title. When the audience was seated on the grounds of the Royal Palace and the traditional *kava* circle formed, a group of women from the Tu'i Lakepa's kinship group and political supporters, entered into the grounds, holding up nearly two dozen brightly colored, machine-made quilts. The red and white banner that led the presentation of *koloa* was, in fact, a stuffed or puff quilt with the name 'Tu'i Lakepa' emblazoned on it attached to two poles for ease of movement and maximum effect for display (see figure 11).

The innovative decision to include the quilts in the presentation of traditional textile wealth was the combined effort of the mother and sister of the new titleholder. The making of the quilts by a group of Tongan women who live in the United States was organised by the

Tu'i Lakepa's sister who lived in the Los Angeles area. Her choice of quilts was based on her inability to acquire the raw materials to produce traditional mats and barkcloth in the United States as well as her aesthetic appreciation of Hawaiian quilts she had seen in Hawai'i and the mainland. Stylistically, the quilts were a mixture of pieced and appliquéd design. As with the quilt *tapu*, traditional Western patterns, Hawaiian-style appliqué, puff quilts, and even a crocheted and appliquéd bedcover were displayed and presented.

Once again, the local Tongan reaction was not entirely positive. While most at the title installation were surprised and delighted with the textile innovation, others believed that it was not *koloa* (traditional Tongan wealth, most often in the form of mats and barkcloth)—at least not of the order of the barkcloth and mats which were also presented that day. There was also uncertainty as to whether the quilts were listed on the official inventory of *koloa* produced that day for the Palace. Most thought that it was considered as a kind of *koloa*, albeit inferior to the more traditional textiles.

Textile wealth (mats and barkcloth) was traditionally, and is still, given to those of higher rank in Tonga as a means of honoring that individual and embodying, in a material thing, the inherent inequality of the relationship between the giver and the receiver. Weiner pointed out that cloth has played such a role in investing political authority in titles and rank throughout the region.[22] As such, the inclusion of quilts at a title installation is culturally appropriate; cloth, even if not traditional cloth, follows rank in Tonga.

In keeping with this practice, the present monarch, H. M. King Taufa'ahau Tupou IV, was presented with an array of textile valuables when he made an official visit to the Laie campus of Brigham Young University on the island of Oahu, Hawai'i, also in 1993. Among his gifts were many quilts, most in a Hawaiian-style appliqué, made by the local Tongan women. In this case, however, the quilts were not presented with the piles of traditional textile wealth or *koloa* during the royal *kava* ceremony, but, instead, were presented at the festivities (including feasting and dancing) which followed. The meaning to the women was obvious—while the quilts were "wealth" and were "valued" they took second place to barkcloth and mats—the traditional forms of textile wealth. They were, in a sense, *koloa si'i* ("little" or "junior" wealth). Their junior or inferior status was clearly demarcated by their exclusion from the *kava* ceremony; although the fact that they were presented to Royalty suggests that they were still considered valuable.

Quilts are beginning to appear as presentations at other significant life events in Tongan communities. Recently in the Kingdom, for example, a dozen cot quilts were sewn and presented, in addition to traditional forms of textile wealth, to a woman at the birth of her daughter by the mother's paternal aunt *(mehekitanga)*. The *mehekitanga* relationship is a very special one in Tongan society and is marked by distinct behavior and gift giving—usually to the *mehekitanga*.[23] Significantly, the new mother's aunt had bitterly argued with her during her pregnancy and the community believed that the quilts, given in large numbers and accompanied by traditional textile wealth, represented the aunt's public desire for reconciliation. Similarly, quilts have begun to appear among wedding presentations; again, along with more traditional forms of textile wealth. They were also displayed and presented to attending royalty in the 1997 combined celebrations marking the 50th wedding anniversary of His Majesty King Taufa'ahau Tupou IV and Queen Mata'aho and the anniversary of the founding of Tonga College.[24]

Quilts and the Tongan Textile Repertoire

Adrienne Kaeppler has argued that the "grammar," or underlying structure, of Tongan art in general follows a three-part conceptual organization similar to that of Tongan music with "melody or leading part *(fasi)*, drone *(laulalo)*, and decoration *(teuteu).*"[25] She developed the argument by demonstrating how the interconnecting parts function in a polyphony to emphasize the relevant features of any Tongan aesthetic or, by identifying the essential feature (through *fasi)*, delimiting its spatial limitations (the function of the *laulalo* or drone), and elaborating its specific features through decoration *(teuteu)*. Kaeppler demonstrated that this organising principle can be seen in the performance of dance *(faiva)*, vocal music *(hiva)*, and the production and decoration of barkcloth *(ngatu)* as well as Tongan kin and gender structures.

When applied to the introduction of appliquéd or pieced quilts into a Tongan notion of wealth as property, Kaeppler's insightful analysis provides a framework for appreciating this introduction as an expansion of traditional Tongan notions of textile wealth. The quilts are encompassed within the traditional textile realm rather than perceived as a deviation from Tongan concepts. The quilts are not seen as a mere foreign influence, but rather as adhering to appropriate Tongan principles. The process is one of transformation and embellishment rather than replacement. Simply stated, the quilts do not seek to supplant or undermine the value of barkcloth or mats; instead, they can be appreciated as a decoration *(teuteu)* of traditional forms of Tongan textile wealth that enhances or shows off the beauty and craft of traditional textiles. The quilts, as previously discussed, embody many of the inherent features of traditional textiles which makes them part—a junior part—of the Tongan conception of textile wealth. Barkcloth and fine mats remain the most valuable and cherished textiles in Tonga.

This process was clearly exemplified at the presentations of quilts to the King during the title installation of the Tu'i Lakepa and also at the festivities following the Royal *kava* ceremony in Hawai'i. In both instances, the quilts were presented *in addition to*, not in place of, traditional forms of textile wealth. In each case, barkcloth and fine mats remained as the essential feature of the presentation; the quilts enhanced the qualities of these items by duplicating and elaborating them in a lesser or junior form—*koloa si'i*, ("little" or "junior" wealth). The quilts supported and celebrated the principal textile wealth by drawing the audience's attention to the fineness of the textiles. The quilts acted as *teuteu* ("decoration"). In neither case is it the intent of the quilts—the *teuteu*—to displace or replace the essential feature—the traditional textiles; rather they are to support their preeminence and add to their prestige. They do not disrupt the concept of "wealth" but mimic it in a form of hybridization congruent with traditional cultural ideals. The effect is one of transformation and creative play with notions of wealth as well as the enhancement of traditional values rather than one of substitution or foreign hegemony.

What is also abundantly clear in this creative adaptation of tradition is the place of the Tongan diaspora in a modern reckoning of Tongan identity.[26] The impetus for creating quilts as *koloa si'i* came from Tongan women living overseas, mostly in the United States. It allowed these women to participate in presentations to kin relations in Tonga in culturally appropriate ways. The cloth, manipulated and, in a sense, re-constructed by the patchwork or appliqué process, held on to the intrinsic nature and value of traditional textile wealth, while also allowing for innovation based on their modern situation. This allowed each woman to negotiate and translate her cultural identity as well as her new geographical surroundings through the traditional female domain of textiles. The quilts encompass the experience of contemporary Tongans in a modern globalized society. The hybrid textiles produced—the quilts—represent the transculture reality of Tongans today—at once traditional and modern, Tongan and Western. A combination of technology, creativity, and purpose has produced an item both unique and familiar; unique in that a clear Tongan quilt style or aesthetic is emerging, yet familiar because this quilt style fits into a traditional textile framework. In each case, migrant Tongan women could have solved their presentation dilemma through the commodification of textile wealth—they could have bought or arranged with relatives in Tonga to buy bales of barkcloth or appropriate mats. These women, however, chose to decline commodification in these cases (I am not saying they would always do this) and, instead, to reinvent how Tongan women express their identity, meet their commitments, and display their culture.

The creation of quilts and bed coverlets appeals to the aesthetics of Tongan women for a number of reasons: the colors, the juxtaposition of fabrics, and the very fact that the quilts are textiles present the possibility of a technological and ideological hybridity within Tonga notions of textile wealth. In addition, the manipulation and processing of the cloth to make it into something new is significant to the quilters. This process connects the women to the valued textile heritage of Tonga and, as Weiner points out, to the textile heritage throughout Oceania.[27] The fact that the quilts also celebrate kin connections overseas adds to their attraction. Quilts are assuredly part of the evolving modern textile repertoire of Tongan women. The richness and depth of the Tongan textile heritage is reflected in the creativity and innovation that Tongan women bring to this new textile art form. Their chosen design applications and color combinations suggest an emerging Tongan style of quilting—an innovative aspect of the wealth of Tongan women's textiles.

Acknowledgment

Research for this project was graciously and generously supported by grants from the Marsden Fund of the Royal Society of New Zealand and the University of Auckland Research Committee. I would also like to thank Adrienne Kaeppler and Jehanne Teilhet-Fisk for thoughtful discussions and helpful advice as well as the anonymous readers for their suggestions and corrections. An earlier version of this paper was presented at the New Zealand Association of Social Anthropologists Conference, Auckland, August 1999.

Notes and References

1. See Phyllis S. Herda, "The Changing Texture of Textiles in Tonga," *Journal of the Polynesian Society* 108:2 (June 1999): 149–67.

2. See Patrick V. Kirch, *The Evolution of the Polynesian Chiefdoms* (Cambridge: Cambridge University Press, 1984).

3. See Simon Kooijman, *Tapa in Polynesia* (Honolulu: Bernice P. Bishop Museum, 1972).

4. See Geoffrey Irwin, *The Prehistoric Exploration and Colonisation of the Pacific* (Cambridge and Melbourne: Cambridge University Press, 1992).

5. See Janet Davidson, "Western Polynesia and Fiji: The Archaeological Evidence," *Mankind* 11:3 (1978): 383–90; Adrienne Kaeppler, "Exchange Patterns in Goods and Spouses: Fiji, Tonga and Samoa," *Mankind* 11:3 (1978):246–52.

6. See Elizabeth Bott, "Power and Rank in the Kingdom of Tonga," *Journal of the Polynesian Society* 90:1 (March 1981):7–81; M. D. Sahlins, *Social Stratification in Polynesia*, American Ethnographical Society Monograph 29 (Seattle: University of Washington Press, 1958); I. Goldman, *Ancient Polynesian Society* (Chicago: University of Chicago Press, 1970) .

7. See Robert Langdon, "The Maritime Explorers," in *Friendly Islands: A History of Tonga*, ed. Noel Rutherford (Melbourne: Oxford University Press, 1977) 40–62; and Niel Gunson, "The Coming of Foreigners" in Ibid., 90–113.

8. See Sione Latukefu, *Church and State in Tonga: The Wesleyan Methodist Missionaries and Political Development, 1822–1875* (Canberra: Australian National University, 1974).

9. Tongan migration is discussed in Wendy E. Cowling, "Motivations for Contemporary Tongan Migration," in *Tongan Culture and History,* eds. Phyllis Herda, Jennifer Terrell, and Niel Gunson (Canberra: Australian National University, 1990), 187–205; and Edgar Tu'inukuafe, "Tongans in New Zealand," in Ibid., 206–14; and Cathy A. Small, *Voyages: From Tongan Villages to American Suburbs* (Ithaca: Cornell University Press, 1997).

10. Ibid., 4; Statistics New Zealand, *New Zealand Official Yearbook 1997* (Wellington: GP Publications, 1997), 124.

11. Norman Douglas, "'Unto the Islands of the Sea': The Erratic Beginnings of Mormon Missions in Polynesia, 1844–1900," *Gods Many, Visions of God*, eds. Phyllis Herda, Michael Reilly and David Hilliard (manuscript in preparation).

12. See Niel Gunson, *Messengers of Grace: Evangelical Missionaries in the South Seas, 1797–1860* (Melbourne: Oxford University Press, 1978), 274–76; see also Bonnie Maywald, "Women of the Lotu: The Foundations of Tongan Wesleyanism Reconsidered," in *Tongan Culture and History*, 118–33.

13. Annette B. Weiner and Jane Schneider, *Cloth and Human Experience* (Washington and London: Smithsonian Institution Press, 1989), 3.

14. Annette B. Weiner, "Why Cloth? Wealth, Gender and Power in Oceania," in Weiner and Schneider, 63.

15. Jehanne Teilhet-Fisk, "Tongan Grave Art," in *Art and Identity in Oceania*, eds. F. Allan and Louise Hanson (Honolulu: University of Hawaii Press, 1990), 222–43; see also Adrienne Kaeppler, "Me'a Fala'eiki," in *The Changing Pacific: Essays in Honour of H. E. Maude*, ed. Niel Gunson (Melbourne: Oxford University Press, 1978), 174–202.

16. Many thanks to Adrienne Kaeppler and Jehanne Teilhet-Fisk for bringing this to my attention.

17. Stella M. Jones, *Hawaiian Quilts* (Honolulu: Honolulu Academy of the Arts, 1930, reprint, 1973).

18. Weiner and Schneider, 3.

19. Herda, 153–56.

20. Teilhet-Fisk, 231–33.

21. For a discussion of the *kava* ceremony see E. E. V. Collocott, "Kava Ceremonial in Tonga," *Journal of the Polynesian Society* 36 (1927): 21–47; and Elizabeth Bott, "Psychoanalysis and Ceremony: A Rejoinder to Edmund Leach," in *The Interpretation of Ritual: Essays in Honour of A. I. Richards*, ed. J. S. La Fontaine (London: Tavistock Publications, 1972), 205–37; 277–82.

22. Weiner, 62–3.

23. See Garth Rogers, " 'The Father's Sister is Black': A Consideration of Female Rank and Powers in Tonga," *Journal of the Polynesian Society* 86:2 (June 1977): 157–82.

24. Many thanks to Adrienne Kaeppler for bringing this to my attention.

25. Adrienne Kaeppler, "Melody, Drone and Decoration: Underlying Structures

and Surface Manifestations in Tongan Art and Society," in *Art in Society: Studies in Style, Culture and Aesthetics*, eds. Michael Greenhalgh and Vincent Megaw (London: Duckworth, 1978), 261–74.

26. See Homi K. Bhabha, *The Location of Culture* (London and New York: Routledge, 1994); Néstor Garcia Canclini, *Hybrid Cultures: Strategies for Entering and Leaving Modernity* (Minneapolis: University of Minnesota Press, 1995).

27. Weiner, 63.

"Better Choose Me": Addictions to Tobacco, Collecting, and Quilting, 1880–1920

Ethel Ewert Abrahams and Rachel K. Pannabecker

Some of the most unusual textiles in American quiltmaking are fabric novelties promoting tobacco consumption in the late-nineteenth and early-twentieth centuries. These novelties include silk ribbons wrapped around cigars as well as printed silk fabrics and cotton flannels that were inserted in tobacco packaging or distributed as premiums. This research used tobacco industry history, information from women's magazines, and tobacco novelty quilts to explore the cigar-ribbon quilt which emerged as a grassroots creation using textiles publicizing cigar brands, the "silkie" quilt which was made from collectible novelties distributed as part of competition in the cigarette industry, and the tobacco flannel quilt which was explicitly encouraged in tobacco advertising aimed at women. In summary, tobacco novelty quilts represent the intersection of American commerce, advertising, and consumer choices during the "age of abundance."

The 1980s and 1990s have been recognized as decades of conspicuous con-sumption with brand names and designer labels proliferating in the American marketplace. Ironically, the phrase "conspicuous con-sumption" was coined a century earlier by an eccentric sociologist, Thorstein Veblen. Veblen sought to characterize how newly rich Americans displayed their wealth, particularly through wasteful purchases of clothing, food, furniture, and houses.[1]

Veblen's period, the late-nineteenth and early-twentieth centuries, is now interpreted by cultural historians as representing the "culture of abundance" or the "culture of consumption."[2] These terms signify the explosion of manufactured goods purchased by Americans, a lifestyle of buying that resulted from the transition from an agricultural to an industrially based economy, and the accompanying "shift from a producer to a consumer culture."[3]

For quilt lovers, the crazy quilt is the epitome of the age of abundance. Constructed of rich materials such as silk jacquards, satins, and velvets, with embellishments ranging from fanciful embroidery to miniature painted motifs, the crazy quilt exemplified both the maker's access to luxury fabrics and the leisure time to ornament her home.[4] Yet, as noted by quilt historians Virginia Gunn and Dorothy Cozart, the crazy quilt was not restricted to upper-class homes.[5] Because of its scrappy structure, a crazy quilt was within the reach of any woman with access to scraps of fine fabric and the determination to make her own fashionable quilt.

The renaissance of American quilting in the last quarter of the twentieth century has revived interest in and appreciation for the asymmetrical designs and technical artistry of crazy quilts.[6] Yet the popularity of this distinctively American-style quilt has obscured the story of another quilt from the age of consumption: the tobacco novelty quilt.[7]

"Better Choose Me":
Brand Names and the Cigar-Ribbon Quilt

The cigar industry grew significantly in the 1870s and in the 1880s the cigar became the most popular tobacco product in the United States.[8] Cigars were rolled by hand, and production could be housed in large New York City com-panies employing immigrant labor, in family-based craft shops in Lancaster County, Pennsylvania, and in small "factories" located in almost every state (which we might think of only as retail tobacco shops). As a decentralized industry, these independent producers sold mostly to local markets.[9]

During the rise of cigar popularity, silk ribbons were wrapped around bundles of cigars, a custom originating in Cuba. These ribbons, made of lower-quality silk in a low-count, plain weave, were lustrous enough to attract attention, and sufficiently stable to be printed with the cigar's brand name in black or red. While they often appeared in tones of yellow and orange, cigar ribbons were also produced in black, blue, green, pink, purple, red, and white.[10] Several cigar brands, including Harvard and Electric, featured ribbons with higher grade silk and woven-in names.[11]

The decentralization of cigar manufacturing and the absence of a nationwide marketing system led to the proliferation of brand names. Branded products were widespread in the tobacco industry, dating back to the early-seventeenth century, and preceded other forms of advertising.[12] Cigar brands ranged from Spanish names that evoked the preferred Cuban tobacco (e.g., Reina Victoria, Caballeros) to all-American names (e.g., Banker's Daughter) or a slogan such as "Better Choose Me" from the BCM Company that also touted its product as the "Best Cigar Made."[13] Ultimately, the goal of branding was to encourage purchasing loyalty in an industry where the competing products were not highly distinctive. Pamela Laird, a historian of advertising, proposed that the economic crash of 1893 heightened the worth of these trademarks.[14] At the turn of the century, some 350,000 different cigar brands were available in the United States.[15] According to Nannie M. Tilley, a tobacco historian, the "plethora of different brands testifies that the value of a brand was recognized."[16]

The abundance of cigars, obviously a totally consumable product, paralleled the abundance of non-consumables which could be collected and displayed. The advent of collecting by average Americans is illustrated by the collecting craze for advertising novelties sparked by the distribution of manufacturers' trade cards at the 1876 Centennial Exhibition in Philadelphia.[17] This mania for collecting extended to cigar ribbons and eventually to the display of one's collection in a quilt or in other decorative items such as table covers or pillow tops.[18]

Cigar-ribbon quilts show both similarities to and differences from the crazy quilts of the same era. Like crazy quilts, cigar-ribbon quilts were ornamental and destined for the parlor. Like the crazy quilt, the cigar-ribbon parlor throw in Figure 1 was created by stitching the ribbons onto a muslin foundation. In contrast to the kaleidoscope of shapes and textures in a crazy quilt, the rectangular form of the ribbon was preserved by the makers through geometric arrangements. Yet the makers frequently recognized the design potential of

Figure 1. Silk Quilt, ca. 1880s. Silk cigar ribbons; herringbone stitching; replacement binding and backing. Maker unknown; purchased in Ohio. Photograph courtesy of Kauffman Museum.

the printed brand name. For example, the maker of the throw in Figure 1 staggered the black printing on every other row. Given the fragility of the silk surface, neither crazy nor cigar-ribbon quilts were actually quilted, nor have we found any cigar-ribbon quilts using a batting. Like crazy quilts, cigar-ribbon quilt seams were embellished with embroidery, often in black to repeat the black printing in contrast to the yellow silk. The simple herringbone stitch, seen in Figure 1, or the feather stitch were most common.

Dating cigar-ribbon quilts is an uncertain task which has been guided largely by collectors of tobacciana.[19] The earliest link between cigar ribbons and quiltmaking comes from a story appearing in an 1884 issue of *Godey's Lady's Book* in which a young woman *rejects* her brother's offer of "nasty little yellow cigar ribbons" for her crazy quilt.[20]

Not until 1896 do cigar ribbons appear in print as useful materials for sewing. In a column of advice from "Honorine" in *The Cultivator & Country Gentleman*, a shopper searching for the perfect gift for her husband is told: "You have heard of the craze for collecting cigar ribbons . . . why not beg, borrow or steal enough to ornament a smoking table?" The column then included directions for a "brier-stitched" table cover with ball fringe of yellow silk, a covered cigar box, and a tobacco pouch, all made of cigar ribbons. Honorine had opened her column with instructions for creating a sofa cushion made of cigar ribbons, noting that the "black lettering and yellow ribbons form a striking contrast."[21]

The notion that cigar ribbons could be both collectible and useful was echoed in the February 1900 issue of *The Housekeeper*:

> If the men of the family or of your acquaintance will smoke, it is some compensation to know that you can make a unique and really handsome pillow from the cigar ribbons which you may thus collect. The pillow is especially appropriate for a bachelor's rooms, a smoking den or library, and it is remarkably effective anywhere.[22]

The instructions for creating a cigar-ribbon pillow on a muslin foundation and the line drawing of a log cabin variation reinforce the links to quiltmaking and suggest that cigar-ribbon creations may have had their origins in the silk log cabin quilts which were popular in the

1870s.[23] The center portion of the design featured in *The Housekeeper* is seen in the table cover shown in Figure 2.[24]

Later that year, the September 1900 issue of *Ladies' Home Journal* published photographs of fourteen pillows submitted for a competition, including one similar to the pattern in *The Housekeeper* but "finished with a ruffle of yellow silk edged with white." A second photograph showed a "sofa-pillow of cigar ribbons in shades of yellow, put

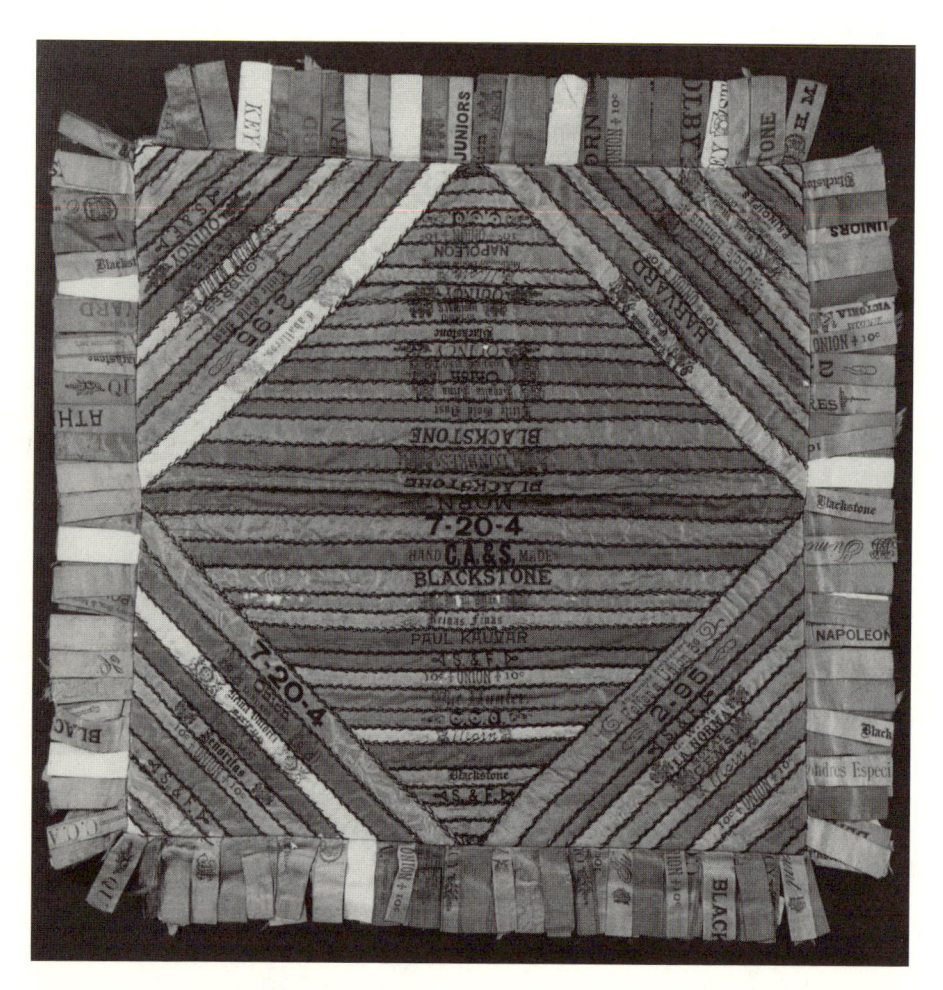

Figure 2. Log Cabin Variation Table Cover, ca. 1880s. Silk cigar ribbons; feather stitching; silk backing. Maker unknown; purchased in Colorado. Photograph courtesy of Kauffman Museum.

together with fancy stitches in yellow silk. The edge was finished with a deep yellow silk cord."[25]

Not everyone appreciated the collectibility and creative potential of cigar ribbons. In response to a query from Little May of Waco, Texas, the editor of *American Woman* stoutly declared in May 1903: "I really do not think pillow-tops made of cigar ribbons at all pretty; but if you have a quantity and wish to use them, do so by all means—it is simply a question of taste."[26] With aesthetics in mind, the editor noted that the brand name was a decorative feature to be manipulated: "Only that portion of the ribbons are used which show the trademark, or name of the cigars which were tied by them." The editor also disclosed her preference for the log cabin arrangement over the "fan" pattern. The two designs must have continued to circulate; six years later both were described by a reader of *Happy Hours*, Wilma B. of Tombstone, Arizona, whose contribution was published in the October 1909 issue.[27]

While colorful paper bands around individual cigars began displacing cigar ribbons in the late-nineteenth century, quilt historian Wilene Smith has discovered magazine correspondence that reveals a lively trade in cigar ribbons throughout the first decade of the twentieth century:

American Woman, February 1901—"Seeds of the beautiful moon-flower, for pieces of silk or yellow cigar-ribbons." (Mrs. D. Gospodich, Los Angeles, California)

Hearth and Home, June 1902—"Silk cigar-ribbons, for same." (Alice Pullen, San Francisco, California)

Sunshine for Youth, April 1906—"Will all the sisters please send me cigar ribbons for my sofa pillow. I will be glad to return the favor in any way I can." (Miss M. Comstock Woodbury, Bangor, Maine)

Hearth and Home, June 1911—"One hundred and sixty silk cigar-ribbons, large handbag, for best offers; write." (Mrs. Mildred Avery, Chimacum, Washington)

Hearth and Home, November 1911—"Hand-embroidered waist, never worn, dry-goods, or other articles, for cigar ribbons; write first, stating what you have and want." (Mrs. E. H. Burghardt, Stevenson, Washington)

Hearth and Home, December 1911—"I should like to receive cigar-ribbons with which to make a sofa-pillow." (Emma Chapman, Roylyn, South Dakota)[28]

Clearly the desire to collect and create with cigar ribbons remained popular across the United States well into the twentieth century.

While 1896 is the earliest published date for sewing with cigar ribbons, we believe that the design links to crazy and silk log cabin quilts support an earlier beginning for cigar ribbon quilts. Following Virginia Gunn in her interpretation of crazy quilts, we propose that the instructions printed in popular women's magazines "followed rather than led" this quiltmaking trend.[29]

Cigar-ribbon quilts should be understood as a creative response to free materials intended to promote brand name recognition among the numerous cigars available across the United States. Given the magazine exchange on collecting and creating with these branded silk ribbons, cigar-ribbon quilts appear as a true grassroots decorative art with no indication that tobacco companies were aware of or promoted their making.

"Each One Recommends One More":
Chain Buying and the Silkie Quilt

In the late-nineteenth century, American cigarette production lagged behind that of the more popular cigar, with bitter competition among small manufacturers.[30] Rival cigarette firms relied on novelties to promote "continuous patronage."[31] During the 1880s, firms began to insert small lithographed cards into cigarette packaging.[32] The free cards, printed in collectible sets, quickly became an industry-wide practice. Tobacco historians consider the cigarette cards as primarily male-oriented, with images of presidents and baseball players as well as female entertainers, often scantily dressed.[33] The educational value of some collectible sets has been pointed out, particularly sets showing flags of the world or mechanical inventions.[34] In an effort to create novelties that would be appealing to women, W. Duke, Sons & Co. distributed coupons redeemable for cards featuring "Costumes of All Nations" which could be collected and glued into a "premium album."[35]

Increasing competition and price-cutting tactics often drove small companies to consolidate with the more aggressive firms, and eventually led to the merger in 1890 of the five largest cigarette manu-

Tobacco Novelty Quilts

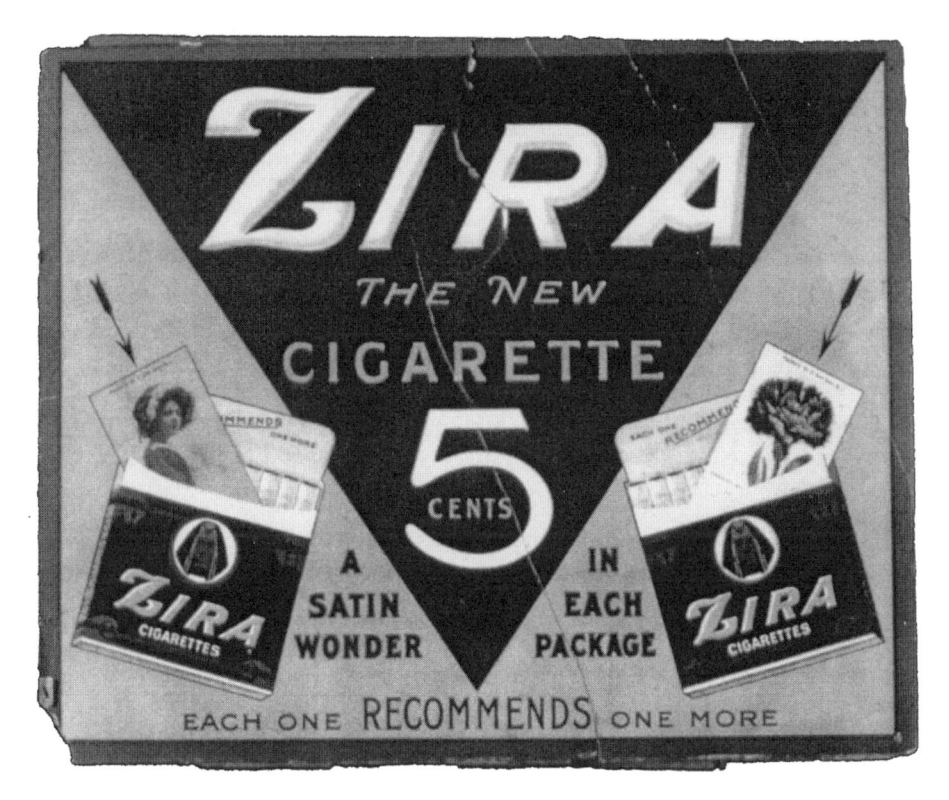

Figure 3. Advertising Poster for Zira Cigarettes, ca. 1914. Photograph courtesy of Gerard S. Petrone.

facturers into the American Tobacco Company. The fad for collecting cigarette cards waned in the 1890s, whether from public disinterest, monopolistic control lessening the pressure to provide incentives to buy, the expense of producing the cards, or the threat of legislation prohibiting packing coupons into product containers.[36]

The decline in cigarette cards paralleled the rather flat numbers for cigarette consumption in the 1890s, with actual declines from 1898 to 1901.[37] Regardless, the new century brought new competition in the form of independently produced cigarettes featuring aromatic Turkish tobacco, and expansion in advertising.[38] Average annual consumption per capita boomed, increasing from 36 cigarettes in 1900–04 to 59 in 1905–09, to 134 in 1910–14, and 310 in 1915–19.[39] Amidst rumors of unfair competition and lawsuits stemming from the Sherman Antitrust Act of 1890, manufacturers introduced a new variation on the prize-in-every package, cigarette silks or "silkies." According to the U.S. Bureau of Corporations, "The great increase in advertising expenditures from 1906 to 1910 was due to newer methods of advertising, such as the insertion of silk banners, flags, novelties, etc."[40]

The size of a cigarette packet, silkies were fabric rectangles made of lightweight all-silk fabric with images printed in black onto light colors such as cream, off-white, or yellow. Early silkies featured portraits of actresses, baseball heroes, and presidents, in poses similar to those found on the earlier cards.[41]

The expansion of cigarette novelties accelerated in 1911 with the break-up of the American Tobacco Company into four companies: American Tobacco, Liggett & Myers, P. Lorillard, and R. J. Reynolds. Cigarette brands from the American Tobacco Company monopoly were divided among the first three firms. This set off a new round of competition for market dominance, and led to the creation of new brands to compete according to price level and tobacco composition. According to Richard Tennant, a tobacco historian, "Although advertising methods remained the same after dissolution, they were greatly developed and expanded. Premiums were made more elaborate. Pictures, souvenir flags, miniature rugs, and other novelties were packed along with cigarettes at considerable cost."[42]

Zira was one of the new cigarette brands formulated after the American Tobacco Company break-up. "Each One Recommends One More," the Zira marketing slogan in 1914, reflected the Lorillard company's promotion of chain buying (see figure 3).[43] The Zira advertising poster also proclaimed "A Satin Wonder in Each Package" and showed an example of an all-silk novelty depicting an actress on the left, and on the right a combination fabric (silk warp and cotton weft) in a satin weave with a multi-colored print of a carnation.[44] The combination fabrics were more colorful than the all-silk versions and also lower in cost to produce.

Packets of Zira cigarettes contained numerous designs issued in collectible sets. The motifs on Zira silkies ranged from flowers to fruit, from queens to American Indians, from domestic to exotic animals, and included a series of cartoon cigarette characters called the Zira girls.[45] Tobacco historian Jack J. Gottsegen has suggested that the designs appealing to children created family pressure to buy more cigarettes.[46] Women incorporated silkies into crazy quilts along with other "found" fabrics, while addicted collectors assembled their accumulated novelties in pillow tops, table covers, and even parlor throws and quilts.[47]

Eventually, Lorillard created a series of thirty-five flags in all-cotton sateen, which were redeemable for Zira and Nebo cigarette coupons rather than being inserted directly into the packaging.[48] In comparison to the smaller silkies, the six by nine-inch cotton novelties could be stitched more easily into a quilt. An unknown quiltmaker sewed her collection of forty-nine flags representing twenty-seven nations into a quilt (see figure 4). The red, white, and blue borders change to bold tricolored stripes on the reverse side.

In contrast to the inexpensive silkies or "satin wonders" issued with modestly priced brands, so-called "luxury" brands of cigarettes distributed silkies which were jacquard-woven silk ribbons with neat selvages. The smoking-room throw shown in Figure 5 shows university and college crests, city and nation seals, and Masonic insignias distributed in Egyptienne Luxury and Turkey Red brands of cigarettes.[49]

In addition to encouraging silkie collecting, tobacco companies also directly promoted the fad for creating with silkies. Instructions included with a silkie from Old Mill Cigarettes, circa 1910, stated "Useful in making pillow covers and other fancy articles for home decoration."[50] Other manufacturers suggested making "doilies, sewing bags, belts, parasols, hair bands, belts, lamp shades, pin cushions, dolls' dresses, and door curtains. They could also be sewn into the designs of 'crazy quilts,' table linens and cushion covers."[51]

The numerous ideas distributed with the novelties may explain why fewer correspondents solicited how-to suggestions in early twentieth-century magazines. In the December 1912 issue of *Hearth and Home*, Mrs. MacGregor of Holyoke, Massachusetts, indicated that she had "silk seals" with butterflies, Indian heads, flags of different countries, and larger designs for the centers of the pillows, but wanted directions for making a pillow-top, because "I have vainly tried to obtain such information from many so-called 'high-class' periodicals."[52] The editor, in response, encouraged her to use creative "ingenuity" by tastefully arranging and appliqueing the silkies onto a fabric foundation with a buttonhole stitch.

Figure 4. Flag Quilt, ca. 1914. Cotton sateen novelties; cotton broadcloth borders and backing; hand-quilted. Maker unknown; purchased in Ohio. Photograph courtesy of Kauffman Museum.

Tobacco Novelty Quilts

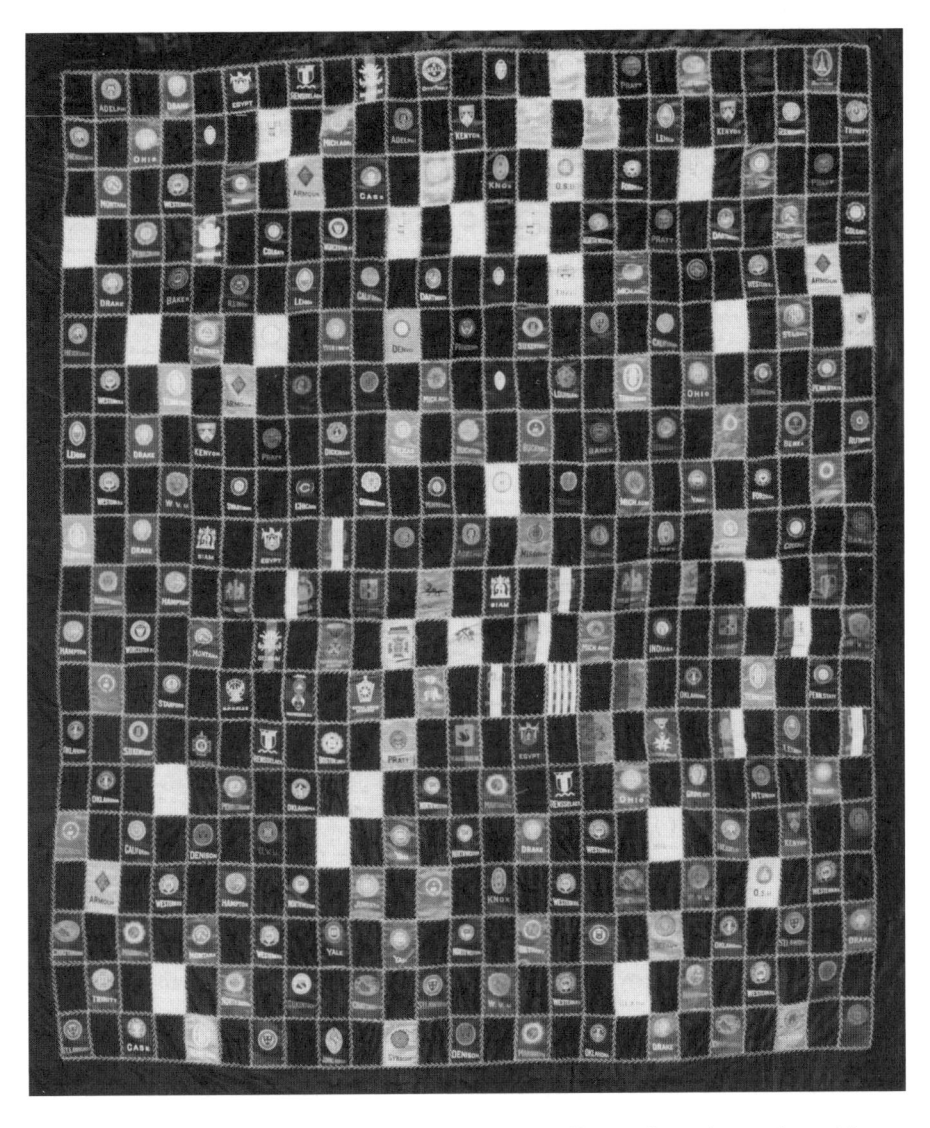

Figure 5. Seals and Crests Parlor Throw, ca. 1912. Silk novelties alternating with silk and cotton fabrics; feather stitching; silk borders; replacement backing; hand-tied. Maker unknown; purchased in Boston, Massachusetts. Photograph courtesy of Kauffman Museum.

Many silkies continued the brand-name promotion established in cigar ribbons. But the brand name, if included on the face of the silkie, was printed or woven along the edge where it could be cut off, covered with decorative embroidery when appliqued, or hidden in a seam allowance if sewn in a patchwork arrangement. Thus the cigarette brand name was literally peripheral to the novelty.

With cigarette silkies, tobacco companies encouraged intentional collecting through repeat purchases, and by extension an addiction to smoking. The collectible set became the significant feature as cigarette companies sought to encourage chain buying over mere brand promotion.

"The Ladies Will Go Wild":
Advertising and the Tobacco Flannel Quilt

The explosion of fabric novelties issued after the break-up of the American Tobacco Company monopoly also included all-cotton printed flannels. Flannels ranged in size from small 2" x 4" models to 8" x 11" pieces or larger. They were distributed as an insert, wrapped around a packet, given away by retailers as a reward for a tobacco purchase, or redeemed with package coupons. The flannels, printed in multiple colors to resemble miniature oriental rugs and the geometric designs found in American Indian blankets, were sometimes called "rugs" and "blankets."[53] One quiltmaker used blue sashing to frame flannels with motifs representing American Indian cultures: Iroquois masks, a peace pipe from a Great Plains Indian tribe, a Pueblo-style kachina, and a totem pole from the Northwest Coast (see figure 6). The swastika is illustrated in many flannels in this pre-World War I quilt. The swastika was an ancient symbol for good health among native Americans as well as for the peoples of India, Iran, and Japan.

Other popular designs on tobacco flannels appearing in quilts include butterflies, college pennants, flags of the world, and Kewpie doll cartoons signed by Rose O'Neill.[54] The bed comforter shown in Figure 7 is signed "May Button, 1912, Chalk Mound" and features a collection of flag flannels, including a United States flag with 48 stars (Arizona and New Mexico joined the union in February 1912 as the forty-

Tobacco Novelty Quilts

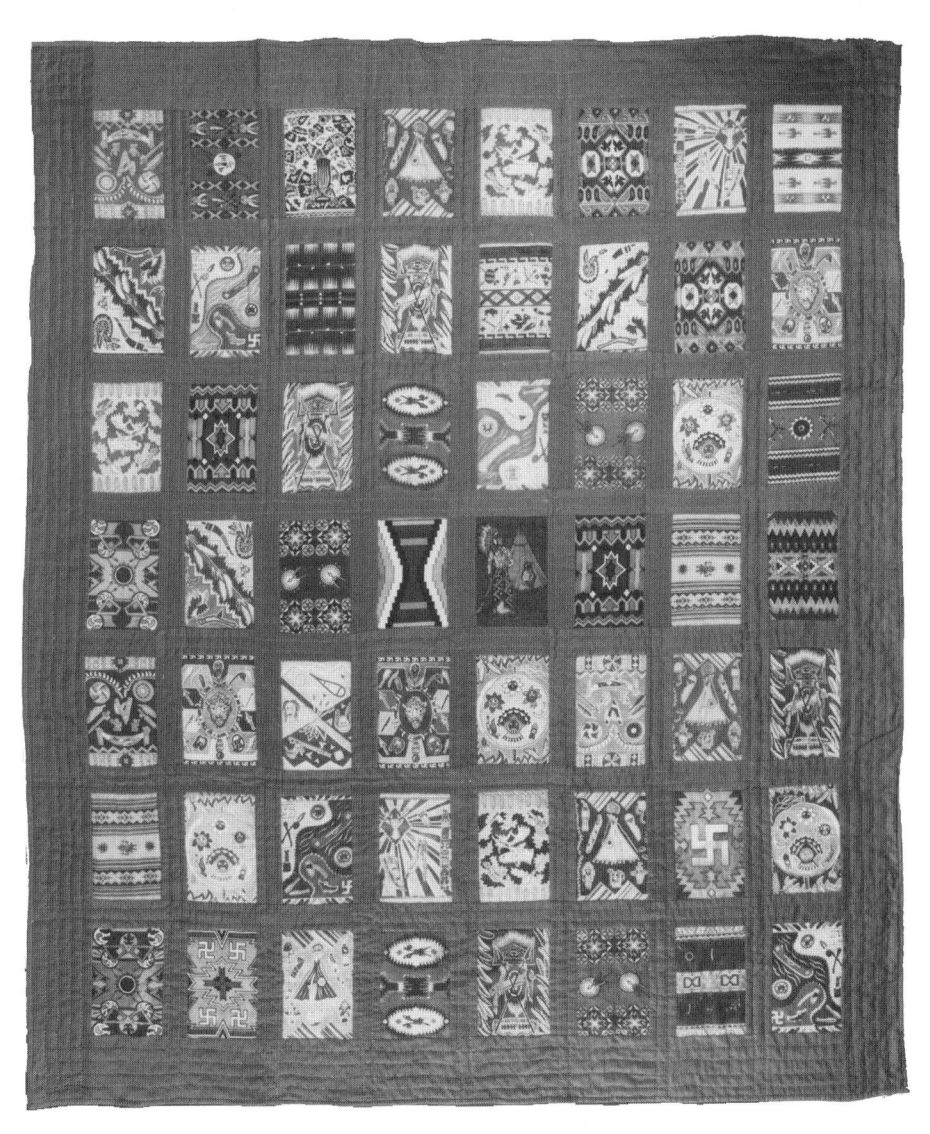

Figure 6. Indian Motif Quilt, ca. 1914. Cotton flannel novelties; cotton twill sashing and border; cotton print backing; hand-quilted. Maker unknown; purchased in Indiana. Photograph courtesy of Kauffman Museum.

Figure 7. Detail of May's Comforter, 1912. Cotton flannel novelties alternating with wool worsted; feather stitching and stem stitch embroidery; cotton blanket batting; striped cotton flannel backing; hand-tied. Makers likely the Chalk Mound, Kansas quilting group; purchased in Kansas. Photograph courtesy of Kauffman Museum.

seventh and forty-eighth states). The heavy comforter was possibly the work of the Chalk Mound, Kansas, quilting group, of which Ida McDivitt Button, May's mother, was a member.

Cathrine Wright (1891–1979) made a baseball flannel quilt for her husband, William. Most flannels were rectangular, so the square flannels printed "on point" to represent a ball diamond are rare (see figure 8). Three flannels in this quilt depict players who were among the first five selected for the Baseball Hall of Fame: Ty Cobb, Walter Johnson, and John P. Wagner. As the owner of a mercantile store in Kansas City, Kansas, William undoubtedly received these flannels to promote tobacco purchases. But since Kansas outlawed the sale or gift of cigarettes in 1909, the Wrights might have preferred to use these

Tobacco Novelty Quilts

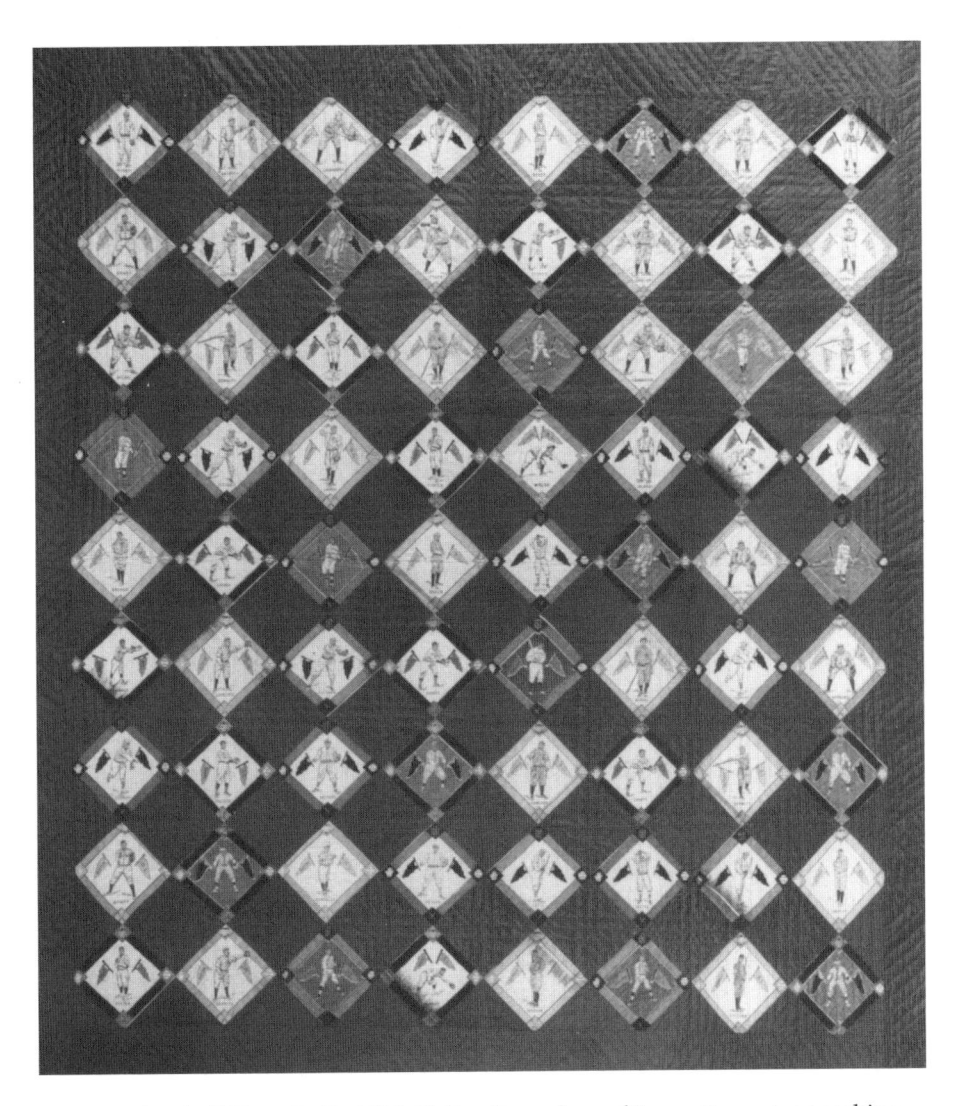

Figure 8. Baseball Hero Quilt, 1916. Cotton flannel novelties; cotton sateen sashing and backing; hand-quilted. Maker Cathrine Wright, Kansas City, Kansas. Photograph courtesy of Kauffman Museum.

cigarette flannels in a quilt for themselves rather than risk prosecution from their distribution.[55]

Most tobacco flannels have no indication of the sponsoring brand, although several with "Satin Cigarettes" stamped on the reverse side have been found.[56] Advertisements from periodicals, however, clearly link the flannels with tobacco purchases (see figure 9). This *Washington Post* advertisement from 24 June 1913 suggested that Navajo blankets were the *"biggest, most marvelous ornamental novelties ever designed! . . . The ladies will go wild with delight over them!"*[57] The 5.5" x 8.5" blankets were distributed with each purchase of a twenty-cigarette packet of Omar, an American Tobacco Company brand introduced in 1912. The advertisement also reveals that the tobacco company targeted women and sought to show them the creative potential of the flannels: "Couch Covers, Den Draperies, Patch Work, Table Covers, Pillow Tops, Navajo Sashes, Fancy Costumes, Dress Trimmings, Doll Blankets, and an endless variety of other useful and ornamental articles."

With tobacco flannels, brand-name promotion and even chain buying were eclipsed in the broader effort to provide a point-of-purchase incentive for buying the tobacco product. Moreover, advertising showing women appeared in the mass media, to encourage product consumption as well as collecting and creating with flannel novelties.

"Our Ingenuity Wore Itself Out": The Demise of Tobacco Novelty Quilts

Collectors and researchers investigating the swift decline of tobacco novelties in the World War I years have proposed that the cost of producing and distributing fabric novelties led tobacco companies to discontinue the giveaways.[58] Yet the major tobacco firms continued to grow steadily until about 1920, suggesting that promotional novelties did not constrain profits.[59] An announcement for Hassan cigarettes in 1914 led to a more complex story. The announcement, made by the premium department of the American Tobacco Company, declared in English, Greek, Italian, and Polish:

Tobacco Novelty Quilts

Figure 9. *Washington Post* advertisement, 24 June 1913.
Image courtesy of Gerard S. Petrone.

SPECIAL NOTICE

We will continue to pack HASSAN Blankets for a short time only, as many of our consumers advise us that they have accumulated a sufficient supply of these Flag Blankets. We will then pack a Valuable HASSAN Coupon which we will redeem for useful presents of unusual value.

"This slip is of no value—and should not be saved"[60]

The notion that the flannels no longer served as an incentive to purchase tobacco was also asserted in a statement by the Bureau of Corporations in 1915:

> The inserts are not desired by many consumers and the coupon system of obtaining articles of merchandise is of somewhat limited value, apparently either because many consumers do not care for these premiums, or because they are not willing to take the trouble to save the coupons and redeem them.[61]

This rationale was echoed by George Washington Hill of the American Tobacco Company who said, "Our ingenuity wore itself out."[62] The availability of alternate premiums, as in the Hassan announcement, and the popular utilization of tobacco novelties by American quiltmakers suggest that other and perhaps less obvious reasons exist beyond the industry-initiated story.

Of the four tobacco companies formed as a result of the break-up of the American Tobacco Company in 1911, only R. J. Reynolds Tobacco Company did not receive a cigarette brand. To establish its position as a major force in the smoking sector, Reynolds launched Camel cigarettes in 1913 and concentrated its advertising on this new brand.[63] The Camel promotional strategy immediately differed from current practice by eliminating novelties. The new package and the mass-media advertising announced: "Don't look for premiums or coupons, as the cost of the tobaccos blended in CAMEL Cigarettes prohibits the use of them."[64] The claim is an example of the "new" sales argument known as the "reason why," which dominated American advertising for much of the twentieth century.[65] Following the introduction of the Camel strategy, the American tobacco industry began to focus on newspaper, magazine, and billboard advertising.[66] According to Richard Tennant, a tobacco historian, "Straight publicity expenditure on a national scale was introduced in place of prizes and premiums."[67]

Tobacco Novelty Quilts

The change in advertising also led manufacturers to drop low volume brands and to concentrate on publicizing their most popular lines.[68]

Other economic and political factors also contributed to the decline of tobacco novelties. The cigarette brands issuing silks and flannels often were tobacco blends which included the aromatic Turkish leaf. Quasi-oriental brand names, such as Hassan, Mecca, Nebo, Omar, or Zira, evoked the Turkish connection. World War I interrupted supplies of Turkish tobacco, driving up the price of the already expensive import.[69] Presumably this price disadvantage led to cost-cutting and the move away from novelties as inserts or premiums. At the same time retail grocery-dealers expressed their opposition to premiums because of lower profits on these goods. States began attempting to prohibit or tax the premium system. Although lower federal courts consistently ruled in favor of allowing premiums, in March 1916 the Supreme Court upheld the right of the states to impose laws governing the distribution of "free" goods.[70] This ruling resulted in state-by-state differences incongruent with the tobacco industry's move towards national marketing. With these changes in the nation's commercial structure, the production and distribution of tobacco novelties simply dissolved.

In the introduction to a book on accumulation and display in American culture from 1880 to 1920, Simon Bronner posed the question: "What arts, customs, and institutions expressed the culture of consumption?"[71] Tobacco novelty quilts tell a unique and underappreciated story of the interaction between American producers and consumers. They provide evidence of how Americans created a "conspicuous" display of their tobacco addiction. They demonstrate that the collecting mania of our time has a parallel a century ago. And they remind us that women creatively respond to materials at hand in their determination to adorn their homes.

Acknowledgments

The authors thank Wilene Smith for sharing her research; Dorothy Cozart and Merikay Waldvogel for their support; Dr. Gerard S. Petrone for contributing images from his tobacciana collection; Greta Hiebert,

Bethel College Interlibrary Loan, for her service; Norman Abrahams, John Pannabecker, and the Kauffman Museum staff for their encouragement; and Kauffman Museum and the Kansas Arts Commission which supported the special exhibition that brought us together for this research.

Publication of this paper was supported by a donation from the Prairie Quilt Guild of Wichita, Kansas.

Notes and References

1. Thorstein Veblen, *The Theory of the Leisure Class* (New York: The Macmillan Company, 1899).

2. Warren Susman, *Culture as History: The Transformation of American Society in the Twentieth Century* (New York: Pantheon Books, 1984), xx; and Richard Wightman Fox and T.J. Jackson Lears, eds., *The Culture of Consumption: Critical Essays in American History, 1880–1980* (New York: Pantheon Books, 1983). Other distinctive labels include age of excess, age of optimism, age of energy, and age of enterprise. See Simon J. Bronner, "Introduction," *Consuming Visions: Accumulation and Display of Goods in America, 1880–1920*, ed. Simon J. Bronner (New York and London: W.W. Norton & Company, 1989), 6.

3. Daniel Horowitz, *The Morality of Spending: Attitudes Toward the Consumer Society in America, 1875–1940* (Baltimore: Johns Hopkins Press, 1985), xxvi.

4. On crazy quilts, see for example, Virginia Gunn, "Crazy Quilts and Outline Quilts: Popular Responses to the Decorative Art/Art Needlework Movement, 1876–1893," in *Uncoverings 1984*, ed. Sally Garoutte (San Francisco: American Quilt Study Group, 1985), 131–52; Virginia Gunn, "Quilts—Crazy Memories," *America's Glorious Quilts*, ed. Dennis Duke and Deborah Harding (New York: MacMillan, 1987), 152–58; Penny McMorris, *Crazy Quilts* (New York: Dutton, 1984); and Paul D. Pilgrim and Gerald E. Roy, *Victorian Quilts, 1875–1900: They Aren't All Crazy* (Paducah, KY: American Quilter's Society, 1994).

5. Gunn, "Crazy Quilts"; Dorothy Cozart, "When the Smoke Cleared," *Quilt Digest 5*, ed. Michael M. Kile (San Francisco: The Quilt Digest Press, 1987), 50–57.

6. See, for example, Judith Montano, *Crazy Quilt Odyssey: Adventures in Victorian Needlework* (Martinez, CA: C & T Publishing, 1991).

7. We define tobacco novelty as an item given away with tobacco purchases. Novelties are also called gratis goods because consumers perceived them as "free." Some novelties were inserted into tobacco packaging and so are called inserts. Other novelties, called premiums, were received after the consumer collected and mailed in package coupons. Sometimes inserts are also called premiums. Tobacco novelties included baseball cards and hand-held fans as well as the fabrics we discuss here. On promotional items in general, see Susan Strasser, *Satisfaction Guar-*

anteed: The Making of the American Mass Market (New York: Pantheon Books, 1989), Chapter 6, "Sales and Promotions."

8. Patricia A. Cooper, *Once a Cigar Maker: Men, Women, and Work Culture in American Cigar Factories, 1900–1919* (Urbana and Chicago: University of Illinois Press, 1987), 12. On the American cigar industry, see also Willis N. Baer, *The Economic Development of the Cigar Industry in the United States* (Lancaster, PA: The Art Printing Co., 1933); Patricia A. Cooper, "What This Country Needs Is a Good Five-Cent Cigar," *Technology and Culture* 29, no. 4 (1988): 779–807; and Meyer Jacobstein, *The Tobacco Industry in the United States* (New York: Columbia University Press, 1907).

9. Jacobstein, 85.

10. Ribbon color is said to differentiate the quality of tobacco, although this remains an oral tradition among collectors. See Cozart, 51.

11. Ibid., 52. Brand names are from cigar-ribbon artifacts in the Ethel Ewert Abrahams Collection which were featured in the exhibition "Better Choose Me: Collecting and Creating with Tobacco Fabric Novelties, 1880–1920" organized by Kauffman Museum in North Newton, Kansas, opening 28 February-3 October 1999, and touring the United States.

12. Jordan Goodman, *Tobacco in History: The Cultures of Dependence* (London and New York: Routledge, 1993).

13. Brand names are from artifacts in the Abrahams collection. A "Better Choose Me/Best Cigar Made" ribbon is shown in Gerard S. Petrone, *Cigar Box Labels: Portraits of Life, Mirrors of History* (Atglen, PA: Schiffer Publishing Ltd., 1998), 69.

14. Pamela Walker Laird, *Advertising Progress: American Business and the Rise of Consumer Marketing* (Baltimore: Johns Hopkins University Press, 1998), 190.

15. Cooper, 1987, 12. Cooper has suggested that national brands emerged with the Robert Burns cigar in 1914 (1988, 783) or the William Penn in 1923 (1987, 310).

16. Nannie M. Tilley, *The Bright-Tobacco Industry, 1860–1929* (Chapel Hill: University of North Carolina Press, 1948), 521.

17. Laird, 77.

18. For examples of cigar-ribbon quilts, see Cozart, 50, 52; Jean Ray Laury, *Ho for California! Pioneer Women and Their Quilts* (New York: E.P. Dutton, 1990), 95–96; Marsha MacDowell and Ruth D. Fitzgerald, eds., *Michigan Quilts: 150 Years of a Textile Tradition* (East Lansing: Michigan State University Museum, 1987), 74; Judith Montano, *Crazy Quilt Handbook* (Lafayette, CA: C & T Publishing, 1986), 8; and Nancyann Johanson Twelker, *Women and Their Quilts: A Washington State Centennial Tribute* (Bothell, WA: That Patchwork Place, 1988), 44–45. Our thanks to Merikay Waldvogel for sharing these references.

19. Jacqueline Key, then curator of the U.S. Tobacco Museum, suggested dating cigar-ribbon quilts from 1875 to the early 1900s ("Silk Cigar Ribbons Turned into Patchwork Quilt," *Greenwich Time*, 31 October 1983, page unknown; clipping supplied by the U.S. Tobacco Museum to Ethel Abrahams). Cozart proposed that cigar ribbons were available as early as 1870, 50. Petrone, page 69, claimed that the "first American cigar ribbon factory was established in 1868 in New York City" and that ribbons were an industry-wide practice by the 1880s.

20. Cited in Cozart, 52. The full story, "The Career of a Crazy Quilt" by Dulcie Weir, is reprinted in Jeanette Lasansky, *In the Heart of Pennsylvania: Nineteenth and Twentieth Century Quiltmaking Traditions* (Lewisburg, PA: Oral Traditions Project, 1985), 80–88.

21. Honorine, "With Cigar Ribbons," *The Cultivator & Country Gentleman*, 2 January 1896, 17. Wilene Smith, a quilt historian from Wichita, Kansas, and member of the American Quilt Study Group, compiled this and following citations from women's magazines as part of a larger research effort on references to quiltmaking in American periodicals.

22. "A Unique Pillow," *The Housekeeper*, February 1900, page unknown.

23. On silk log cabin quilts, see Gunn, "Quilts—Crazy Memories," 153.

24. A larger version of this piecing pattern can be seen in Alexandra Grave, *Three Centuries of Connecticut Folk Art* (New Haven, CT: Art Resources of Connecticut, 1979), 14.

25. "Some Odd Sofa-Pillows," *The Ladies' Home Journal*, September 1900, 25.

26. *American Woman*, May 1903, page unknown.

27. *Happy Hours*, October 1909, page unknown. Smith has noted that the article was reprinted nearly word-for-word in *American Woman*, February 1913.

28. All citations from Smith's unpublished manuscript; see note 21 above.

29. Gunn, "Quilts—Crazy Memories," 155.

30. On the history of the cigarette industry, see Reavis Cox, *Competition in the American Tobacco Industry, 1911–1932* (New York: Columbia University Press, 1933); Goodman; Jack J. Gottsegen, *Tobacco: A Study of Its Consumption in the United States* (New York and Chicago: Pitman Publishing Corporation, 1940); *"Sold American!"—The First Fifty Years* (New York: American Tobacco Company, 1954); Richard B. Tennant, *The American Cigarette Industry: A Study in Economic Analysis and Public Policy* (New Haven, CT: Yale University Press, 1950); and Tilley.

31. "Continuous patronage" was a frequently used term in connection with the premium system. See Strasser, 178.

32. Colorful cigarette cards are shown in Gerard S. Petrone, *Tobacco Advertising: The Great Seduction* (Atglen, PA: Schiffer Publishing Ltd., 1996), 54–57. Tilley, pages 558, 576–77 (footnote 57), credited James B. Duke with introducing cigarette cards. Richard Kluger claimed that earlier cards were issued by the Allen & Ginter Company, in *Ashes to Ashes: America's Hundred-Year Cigarette War* (New York: Alfred A. Knopf, 1996), 18.

33. On sex appeal in cigarette cards, see Patrick G. Porter, "Advertising in the Early Cigarette Industry: W. Duke, Sons & Company of Durham," *North Carolina Historical Review* 48, no. 1 (1971): 31–43. For background on gender and tobacco issues, see Dolores Mitchell, "Images of Exotic Women in Turn-of-the-Century Tobacco Art," *Feminist Studies* 18, no. 2 (1992): 327–42.

34. Porter, 35.

35. *"Sold American!"*, 22. Cigarette companies did not overtly target women smokers until the 1920s. See Gottsegen, 147–50; and Michael Schudson, *Advertising, The Uneasy Persuasion* (New York: Basic Books, 1984), Chapter 6, "The Emergence of New Consumer Patterns: A Case Study of the Cigarette."

36. On monopoly in the cigarette industry, see Tennant, 57; on cost, see Porter, 41, Strasser, 172, and Tennant, 24, 42; and on legislation, see Strasser, 176, and Tennant, 42. Understanding the decline of cigarette cards is beyond the scope of this study but clearly warrants a more complex investigation. On the rise and fall of the trade card in general, see Robert Jay, *The Trade Card in Nineteenth-Century America* (Columbia: University of Missouri Press, 1987).

37. Gottsegen, 26, 28.

38. William H. Nicholls, *Price Policies in the Cigarette Industry* (Nashville: Vanderbilt University Press, 1951), 35; and Tennant, 57.

39. Nicholls, 8; see also Gottsegen, 27–28.

40. U.S. Bureau of Corporations, *Report of the Commissioner of Corporations on the Tobacco Industry, Part III, Prices, Costs, and Profits* (Washington, DC: Government Printing Office, 1915), 165.

41. Like cigar ribbons, the dating of cigarette silkies remains uncertain. Sports memorabilia collectors have suggested 1909 as the earliest date for "white" silkies of baseball players and 1910 for silkies of dyed fabrics, as distributed by Helmar, Old Mill, Red Sun, and Turkey Red brands; Mark K. Larson, *Complete Guide to Baseball Memorabilia* (Iola, WI: Krause Publications, 1996), 394–95. A four-by-six inch silkie with a printed flag was redeemed from Egyptienne Straights cigarettes by Miss L. Jensen of Cheney, Washington in 1911 and the enclosed instruction sheet gave design and project ideas (Francine Kirsch, "The Fanciest of Printed Fabrics," *The Antique Trader Weekly*, 28 March 1990, 85). A similar flag in an envelope dated 1912 is shown in Petrone, *Tobacco Advertising*, 165. Joseph C. Robert noted the role of George Washington Hill of the American Tobacco Company in issuing silk flags with "Egyptian Straights" in order to reach a mass market, in *The Story of Tobacco in America* (New York: Alfred A. Knopf, 1952), 257.

42. Tennant, 70–71. We have found information connecting 35 U.S. cigarette brands with silkies, including Fatima (Liggett & Myers), Nebo (Lorillard), and Tokio (American Tobacco Company); see J. R. Burdick, ed., *The American Card Catalog* (Franklin Square, NY: Nostalgia Press, 1988); Larson; and Petrone, *Tobacco Advertising*. During the same time period, Canadian and British tobacco companies also distributed fabric novelties which appear in Canadian quilts. See Burdick, 85; Deborah Cannarella, "Ellis Island Treasures," *Piecework*, 4, no. 5 (1996): 39; and Mary Conroy, *300 Years of Canada's Quilts* (Toronto: Griffin House, 1976), 83–84.

43. The term "chain buying" appears in a photo caption in *Sold American!*, 23.

44. See also Petrone, *Tobacco Advertising*, 166. The Abrahams collection includes a table cover sewed from two lengths of printed silk-cotton yardage featuring uncut Zira silkies.

45. Burdick, 83–85. Examples of the Zira girls are found in the Abrahams collection.

46. Gottsegen, 191.

47. For examples of silkies sewn into pillows and quilts, see Cannarella, 39; Cozart, 54–55; Kirsch, 87; and McMorris, 64–65, 108–109.

48. Burdick, 83.

49. Ibid. Other woven motifs were national arms distributed by Richmond Straight Cut cigarettes, yacht club and college pennants issued with the Twelfth Night brand, and automobile makes (distributing brand unknown); Burdick, 83, 85.

50. From the card backing of an all-silk novelty distributed by Old Mill Cigarettes, Abrahams collection.

51. Petrone, *Tobacco Advertising*, 165.

52. *Hearth and Home*, December 1912, page unknown; from Smith (see footnote 21 above).

53. Tobacco flannels were also called felts, a misnomer; Tony Hyman, "Readers' Questions on ... Tobacciana," *The Antique Trader Weekly*, 15 September 1993, 94–95. More expensive brands of tobacco issued "Miniature Silk Rugs" which were packed in tins of tobacco or redeemable from the company's premium distribution center. See Burdick, 86–87; Cozart, 51; and Petrone, *Tobacco Advertising*, 167. Many of these fringed velvet novelties with oriental-rug designs were used in doll houses and are not considered here as their structure did not make them useful for quilting. For the same reason we do not discuss leather novelties with stamped patterns distributed by Silko and Turkey Red Egyptian cigarette brands. On leather novelties, see Burdick, 86; and Petrone, *Tobacco Advertising*, 167–68.

54. Tobacco flannel quilts are shown in Barbara Brackman, Mary Madden, Rebecca Martin, and Blair Tarr, *Material Pleasures: Quilts from the Kansas Museum of History* (Topeka: Kansas State Historical Society, 1995), 26; Conroy, 82; Cozart, 53; MacDowell and Fitzgerald, 61 (although the provenance and dating are questionable), 79, 92; and Merikay Waldvogel, "A Flag Quilt Launches a Search into the Past," *Quilting Today*, no. 68, 1998, 26–28. While conventional wisdom among Kewpie collectors holds that these cartoon flannels were issued with tobacco products, others have suggested that they were distributed with gum and candy; Burdick, 87–88.

55. On the Kansas ban on cigarettes, see Petrone, *Tobacco Advertising*, 204; and R. Alton Lee, "The 'Little White Slaver' in Kansas: A Century-Long Struggle Against Cigarettes," *Kansas History*, 22, no. 4 (1999–2000): 258–67.

56. Burdick, 86; Abrahams collection.

57. Advertisement reprinted in Petrone, *Tobacco Advertising*, 167.

58. Cozart, 56; and Petrone, *Tobacco Advertising*, 165.

59. Nicholls, 42–43. Profits of the "successor" companies were, however, relatively lower than before the monopoly break-up, a fact which has been attributed to the large increase in cigarette advertising; U.S. Bureau of Corporations, 328, 444.

60. *"Sold American!"*, 48; illustrated on page 50.

61. U.S. Bureau of Corporations, 379; quoted in Tennant, 83.

62. Tennant, 84.

63. Ibid., 75–78, 82–83; and Tilley, 609–11.

64. Quoted in Tennant, 78.

65. Strasser, 173–74; and Tennant, 77–78.

66. Strasser, 173–74.

67. Tennant, 83.
68. Ibid., 84.
69. Ibid., 79; and Tilley, 611–12.
70. Strasser, 176–79.
71. Bronner, 6.

Hubert Ver Mehren and Home Art Studios

Susan Price Miller

The name Hope Winslow in the title of a 1933 catalog is probably better known than the little recognized man who produced the book and designed some unique twentieth-century pieced quilt patterns. Hubert Ver Mehren of Des Moines, Iowa, marketed his needlework items through magazines, newspapers, and mail-order catalogs. Examination of a dozen newspapers and periodicals and seven versions of his books revealed the growth of Ver Mehren's work in the 1920s and 1930s. The research provides information about some of the by-lines associated with the patterns and shows how Home Art Studios, the title usually associated with the quilt patterns, functioned in relation to Ver Mehren's primary business, the Iowa Button and Pleating Company. The results credit Hubert Ver Mehren with being an artist, entrepreneur, and marketing expert whose name should be attached henceforth to all his original designs.

Introduction: Who Was Hope Winslow?

Who was Hope Winslow, the young woman pictured on page one of *Hope Winslow's Quilt Book* copyrighted in 1933 by Hubert Ver Mehren? Below the photograph she addressed the "fellow-enthusiast" in a letter which closed, "Yours for more and better quilts, Hope Winslow." Her name recalled the American spirit of optimism and the historic Plymouth Colony to people dealing with the Great Depression. She appealed to a post-World War I public that viewed quilts as symbols of the values of the country's founders as well as coverings for the popular early American style beds.[1] At a time when a multitude of pattern producers competed for the quilter's attention in the print media, this cordial Hope Winslow personified the astute marketing strategies of versatile and talented Hubert Ver Mehren, a businessman, entrepreneur, and quilt designer in Des Moines, Iowa.[2]

In the mid-1920s Ver Mehren began stamping embroidery designs on household linens, then turned to producing quilt catalogs, kits, and patterns that built on the quiltmaking tradition and greatly added to it. After trying basic patterns, he soon began to design intricate repeating block layouts and new, unusual, large pieced medallion designs shaded in the popular solid colors of the time. He also created separate complex pieced border patterns that could be added to any of his quilts. His elaborate quilting designs filled and enhanced the open spaces. Quilt authority Cuesta Benberry considers Ver Mehren's pieced medallions "the most ORIGINALLY conceived pieced patterns in the 20th century," equal in originality to Marie Webster's applique designs.[3]

For years quilt historians and pattern collectors have searched for information about these distinctive and original designs. They found clues in the 1933 copyright date, the H. Ver Mehren name, and the Des Moines, Iowa, location printed in very small type inside the front covers of *Hope Winslow's Quilt Book* and one edition of his *Colonial Quilts* book. They compiled lists of newspapers and filed clippings in numerical order. Some even tracked down Mr. Ver Mehren in the 1960s, purchased patterns he still had in stock, and then circulated the originals to be traced by those who wanted copies. A great deal of credit goes to the small groups of collectors in the "Round Robins" of the 1950s and 1960s who found, preserved, and circulated quilt ephemera. Their efforts succeeded in recognizing Ver Mehren as the producer of the patterns which they labeled under the heading "Home Art Studios."[4]

Who was Hope Winslow—and who were Bettina, Carol Dean, Mary Jacobs, Lucretia King, Nancy Lee, and Gertrude May, all names that have been connected with Ver Mehren's patterns? Some were real people, and some were aliases or completely fictitious. These various names have caused confusion and mistaken assumptions for researchers. This paper presents new information about the origin, development, and operation of the Ver Mehren enterprise based primarily on the examination of printed material: six Des Moines-based publications, other newspapers and periodicals, eighteen copies of Ver Mehren's books, several original patterns, and some miscellaneous flyers. The research uncovers the roles or identities of the people involved, both real and imaginary. The results show that the Home Art Studios label does not sufficiently recognize the people connected to that name or credit the individual who created and marketed some of the twentieth century's most original quilt designs.

Hubert Ver Mehren: Background

Hubert Ver Mehren was born August 22, 1892, in Arcadia, Iowa, the home town of his mother whose father, a Dutch immigrant, was the local doctor.[5] The Ver Mehren family actually lived in Omaha, Nebraska, about eighty miles southwest of the tiny rural Iowa town. Hubert's father, Herman Ver Mehren, also of Dutch ancestry, had emigrated from Germany to Nebraska. He married his second wife, Frances, and eventually became president of the Ideal Button & Pleating Company located in Omaha.[6]

After graduating from high school, Hubert Ver Mehren worked for a collection agency before serving as a medic during World War I. He was known as "Van" because of his Dutch heritage, stood six feet tall, and had gray hair by the age of twenty-six. In 1920, he married Mary Ellen Jacobs, his step-mother's younger sister, and moved to Des Moines, Iowa, to manage the *Iowa* Button and Pleating Company (see figure 1).[7] His father was president of the Iowa company while he served as secretary and treasurer for both corporations.[8] The City Office of Iowa Button and Pleating (spelled Plaiting on their catalog) was located at 305 7th Street, about two blocks away from the factory at 202 8th Street. Mary, or "Mayme," Ver Mehren worked as the bookkeeper for the business.[9]

Both the Ideal company in Omaha and the Iowa company in Des Moines dealt with customers by mail through catalogs with identical contents inside different covers.[10] The cover of the *Style Book of Iowa Button & Plaiting Co., Inc.* listed among other items: beading, braiding, buttons, buttonholes, embroidering, eyelets, hemstitching, initials, picot edging, pleating, and scalloping. Inside, under the heading "Stamp-

Figure 1. Mary and Hubert Ver Mehren. Photograph courtesy of Dick Ver Mehren.

ing," the catalog stated: "We stamp all kinds of plain or fancy designs, Borders, Letters, Initials, Monograms of the latest types on Table Cloths, Napkins, Towels, Doilies, Lunch Sets, Waists, Chemises, Corset Covers, Underwear, Baby Clothes, etc., or any article where embroidery could be used.... We can make and stamp monograms of all kinds to order."[11]

The Button and Pleating business prospered in the early 1920s. By mid-decade, the Ver Mehrens had built a new house at 531 Waterbury Circle in Des Moines, and Mary had given birth to a daughter. As changes in clothing styles decreased the demand for some of the fashion services, Ver Mehren began to stamp embroidery designs on linens and quilt blocks. His son was born during the 1928 Iowa State Fair while he was selling Iowa Button and Pleating goods at the fairgrounds.[12]

Ver Mehren and *People's Popular Monthly*

Ver Mehren did not have to go far to find a way to distribute these new products to a larger market. Des Moines, the sixth largest publishing center in the country, was home to numerous farm and family magazines, three of which had more than one million subscribers.[13] One of the three, *People's Popular Monthly*, is virtually unknown now. It played a crucial role, however, in the development of two important pattern providers by giving local talent a chance to reach a national audience. In the early 1920s, Carlie Sexton, the supervisor of the circulation department, had launched her mail-order quilt pattern business and writing career with two signed articles about quilts in the magazine.[14]

In 1926, Kathern Ayres, recently graduated from Iowa State College, joined the staff of *People's Popular Monthly* as the editor of the home pages. To give the appearance of having a larger staff in her department, she adopted the name "Lucretia King" as the by-line for the needlework column.[15] Embroidered pillow cases and a comfort protector photographed on a bed at Younker Brothers, a large department store in Des Moines, illustrated a feature in November 1926. Ver Mehren had produced these linens, as well as a dresser scarf, in a Wild

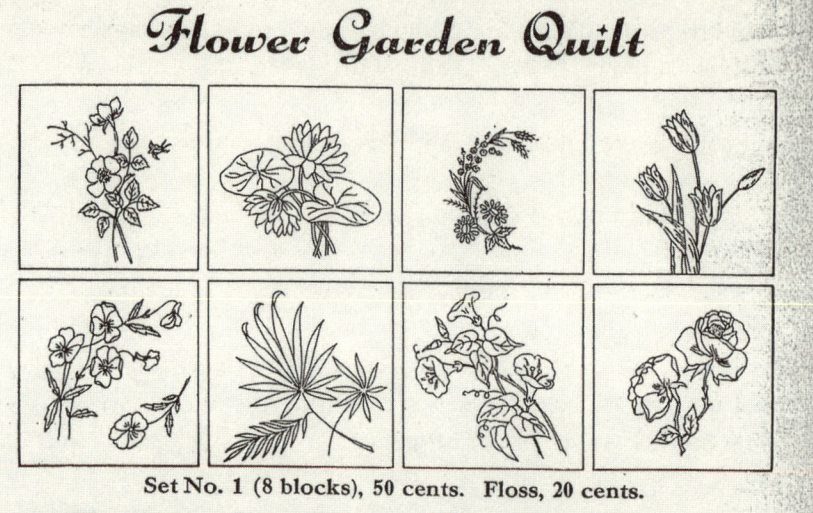

Uncoverings 2000

> # Flower Garden Quilt
>
> Set No. 1 (8 blocks), 50 cents. Floss, 20 cents.
>
> ABOVE are pictured only eight of the 32 blocks which are necessary to complete the quilt. Each block is a different flower design.
>
> The blocks are made of fine white Lonsdale muslin, 9 inches square. They are clearly stamped so that even a child could embroider them.
>
> Set together 32 embroidered blocks with 31 plain or colored blocks, which you supply yourself. This makes a quilt 9 blocks long and 7 wide.
>
> The eight blocks shown above may be ordered at a price of 50 cents or you may have the complete set of 32 blocks for $1.50. Boilfast floss, 6 skeins for 20 cents, or 25 skeins for 75 cents. Name colors wanted. Embroider each flower in its natural colors.
>
> Address Lucretia King, People's Popular Monthly, Des Moines, Iowa.

Figure 2. Eight designs of the thirty-two block set later called "Mother's Old Fashioned Flower Garden" designed by Hubert Ver Mehren. From *People's Popular Monthly*, May 1931. Collection of the author.

Rose design. He would continue to stamp dresser scarves, pillow cases, and quilt protectors in this and many other designs for years to come.

Kathern Ayres and Hubert Ver Mehren worked together in choosing a variety of needlework items for her column. In 1928 "Lucretia King" began offering stamped quilt blocks along with embroidery floss in a variety of colors.[16] She suggested setting the blocks together in an ordinary, standard layout with white or colored strips for sashing and borders. Neither Ayres or Ver Mehren knew much about making quilts although Ayres had seen family members quilting in the front parlor when she was growing up.[17]

The stamped quilt blocks shown in *People's Popular Monthly* were generally of two types. One category consisted of designs executed in cross-stitch. Some of these patterns were similar or identical to products sold by the Ladies Art Company and the Rainbow Quilt Block Company. The second category featured outline-embroidery of natural-looking floral motifs. Kathern Ayres was responsible for some of the flower designs. She copied pictures of flowers and worked out the patterns at a time when copyright issues were not considered.[18] Ver Mehren had natural artistic ability, a characteristic of members of his family before him, and also drew many embroidery designs.[19] *People's Popular Monthly* showed eight blocks of his "Old Fashioned Flower Garden" in May 1930 (see figure 2). In 1931, the Ideal Button & Pleating Company of Omaha copyrighted the Color Chart for all four of the eight-block sets, indicating that Ver Mehren's products belonged equally to the older Omaha business.[20]

Kathern Ayres remembers Ver Mehren as hard working and conscientious, with a good sense about what would sell. He was also willing to carry out her ideas. She suggested, for example, that he provide torn strips of fabrics for quilt borders. Kathern's secretary then assembled all the materials for an order, including rolls of border strips, in a large envelope. An advertising circular always went out with every package. The readers of *People's Popular Monthly* enjoyed the embroidery patterns and especially liked the matching pillow cases and accessories. Simple cross-stitch designs such as Pine Tree and Tulips were popular, and the needlework items made money for the magazine. Pillow cases, for example, sold for $1.28, twice the wholesale price. Management was quite satisfied with the profits and the reader response.[21]

The magazine also used the needlework products to promote circulation. In the January 1930 issue, a small advertisement offered a free Double T quilt pattern to anyone who sent for information about obtaining a free set of cross-stitch blocks. The reader then received a flyer stating the number of new magazine subscriptions that had to be sold in order to earn the extra premium.[22] Soon Ayres and Ver Mehren collected twelve traditional quilt designs from various sources that the magazine listed under "Patchwork Patterns" in February 1931.[23] Five paper patterns cost 25 cents, or stamped fabric for the whole top could be bought for $2.50. Illustrations of the twelve "old-time favorites" debuted in May 1931, the final issue of the magazine.[24] A series of tiny dots formed the lines on Ver Mehren's paper patterns, just like lines stamped on fabric. The printed pattern of number five, Yankee Pride, has a pattern piece of unusual shape which requires snipping the seam allowance to set in the adjoining diamond and shows a lack of knowledge of traditional piecing methods.[25]

During the winter of 1931–1932, Kathern and her husband, Carlton Chase Proper, Jr., the son of the magazine editor, moved to her home town of Wilton Junction in eastern Iowa. In one bedroom of her mother's house, "Lucretia King" continued to fill the orders that customers still addressed to *People's Popular Monthly*. She always included an advertising flyer for more of the Ver Mehren items from her columns.[26]

By 1931, Ver Mehren understood which designs and products appealed to the customers. He had shown he was amenable to suggestions and quick to respond to trends. Most of all, he knew how to merchandise his goods and always followed up a contact with a sales circular for proven staple items. "Lucretia King" provided a feminine presence in the presentation of Ver Mehren's products to the public. The quilts in *People's Popular Monthly* had none of the originality of Ver Mehren's later designs, but the ordinary layouts with simple quilting were successful and easy to complete.

The Briardale Store News

In October 1930, eight months before the end of *People's Popular Monthly*, another Des Moines publication began making quilt patterns available to its readers. The Briardale chain of grocery stores published *The Briardale Store News*, its own monthly newspaper with features about food and homemaking interspersed with advertising. A quilt column continued fairly regularly for at least four years. Although no by-line accompanied the quilt column through the first winter, several factors point to former Des Moines resident, Carlie Sexton, as the writer.

Herbert Ver Mehren/Home Art Studios

The first clue that Sexton authored the Briardale feature is the title "Quaint Old Fashioned Quilts" which combines the words she frequently used in the titles of her books and articles. Secondly, the first column with this name begins with one of her poems and a slight variation of a paragraph in *Old Fashioned Quilts*, published in 1928.[27] Of course, someone could have "borrowed" this material, but how foolish to copy the work of a woman undoubtedly known in quilting circles in Des Moines! The rest of the writing in the column through the spring of 1931 is rough but still characteristic of Sexton's style. At this time her husband's printing business had failed, and her quilt work supported both of them. Writing copy for another Des Moines publication, while Ver Mehren made the patterns, would have been an easy, extra job. The patterns, at first titled simply "Briardale Designs," were from Ver Mehren; they had the same one hundred series numbers as the blocks in his later catalogs.[28]

The early Briardale patterns were common patterns with the illustrations taken straight from the Ladies Art Company catalog pages. Customers bought the patterns through the paper or ordered fabric for a complete top already stamped with the geometric pieces for $1.98 at a Briardale store. A kit for the Lone Star, number 140, in four shades of yellow sateen cost $5.95. A black and white illustration of the star gave little idea of its impressive appearance in cloth, so Ver Mehren used a large color photograph of one-fourth of the actual quilt whenever possible. He pasted the picture to a pattern package copyrighted by Iowa Button and Pleating and sold about this time at Younker Brothers.[29] The department store also printed the picture in a color flyer that advertised sateen fabrics and "paper patterns for quilts."[30]

In September, 1931, the *Briardale Store News* quilt column changed in name and style. Under the name "Carol Dean," it included more quilt patterns but no longer as pre-stamped fabric for the simple pieced blocks. Carol Dean, whose true identity is still unknown, soon offered a catalog of patterns, needlework items, and popular kits and also an album of quilting designs, both Ver Mehren products. With the catalog, quilters had a colorful reminder of all the good things available, ostensibly, through Briardale. The direction to "read the Art Needlework Book offer on page 7" in September 1931 is the earliest notice found so far for *Colonial Quilts and Decorative Needle Work*. Carol Dean and the Briardale Stores persuaded quilters to buy "their" book for twenty-five cents by including a free quilt pattern of the customer's choice that usually cost ten cents.[31]

Ver Mehren's Catalogs—The Contents

Today's quilters may have seen some of the vintage booklets that Hubert VerMehren created for the mail-order sale of his products. Few probably know the true source of the books or realize there were at least seven different versions.[32] The striking appearance of the catalogs, with pages printed in orange and yellow, orange and green, green and purple, and orange and dark turquoise, could easily capture a quilter's attention then and now.

The earliest version of *Colonial Quilts and Decorative Needle Work*, however, did not have color printing or the polish of the later books. This sixteen-page edition in black and white, dating from about 1930, began with quilt patterns derived from the Ladies Art Company and numbered from 101 to 134. Nine pages featured stamped aprons, baby dresses, bedroom sets, curtains, pictures, quilt blocks, rayon pillows and and wool felt silhouette pillows. The catalog also included such non-needlework products as "Chardonez" rayon undergarments, silk hose, and window curtains.[33]

The sixteen-page version of *Colonial Quilts and Decorative Needle Work* with colored illustrations eliminated the curtains, garments, and most of the stamped goods in favor of more attractive pages of quilt patterns. It can be docu-mented from the fall of 1931 through the spring of 1932.[34] Three versions with the shorter title *Colonial Quilts* and a George Washington Mount Vernon Quilt on the back cover were also from 1932.[35] The first version sold just the patterns illustrated on the twenty-four pages. The next one expanded to thirty-two pages and listed additional patterns numbered from 200 to 253. The third version added more 200–series patterns to the list, including some for applique. Ver Mehren's name and the copyright date of 1933 appeared inside the front cover of a fourth *Colonial Quilts* which advertised "Aunt Dinah's Quilting Album" on the outside of the back cover. It repeated the previous layout of pages, but the colors differed, the

Figure 3. Covers of two of Ver Mehren's catalogs, from the author's collection.

pattern list included a few 300–series numbers, and the edges of the pages had been trimmed down to 5.5 x 8.5 inches. The same size *Hope Winslow's Quilt Book*, also from 1933, had different pages and colors but an identical list of patterns as *Colonial Quilts* (1933) except for an extra fourth digit in the identifying number (see figure 3).[36]

Taken in order, the catalogs reveal the development of Ver Mehren's designs and his business. His Lone Star quilt was instrumental in both spheres. From the beginning of his foray into quilt patterns, he promoted the distinctive Lone Star design in solid shades of one color.

Page one of the very first catalog attributed the pattern to the skillful fingers of Betsy Ross, and suggested using "four shades of yellow, pink, orchid or blue."[37] Perhaps it should have attributed the layout of the colors and the border composed of four narrow bands to Carlie Sexton. In 1923, she published a black-and-white photograph of her own Lone Star quilt with the words "Four colors or four shades of one color must be used."[38] Her connection to the Briardale column and patterns may indicate an association with Ver Mehren and the development of his star quilt.

The first 1932 *Colonial Quilts* catalog included Ver Mehren's color photograph of the Lone Star in shades of yellow and orange with clearly visible quilting making the soft texture of the sateen palpable. The same colors also worked very effectively in the companion picture of the Rising Sun quilt. Edged with four narrow border strips, this large single central motif was a somewhat more elaborate version of Ladies Art Company block number 266, Slashed Star. In these large medallion patterns, stamped fabric for pieced designs was put to its best use. The medallions required careful selection of fabric, and the kits supplied the most stylish colors and fabrics that one might not otherwise buy. They were economical in terms of fabric and labor. With the Lone Star the quilter was spared endless tracing around the same diamond template. The Rising Sun kit avoided tracing very large, complex shapes requiring great accuracy. Both considerations applied to the Star of France Quilt, photographed in three different colorways —yellows, pinks, and blues—for different editions of the catalogs.

In the second version of *Colonial Quilts*, different borders on several embroidered quilts departed from the previous straight edges. Gentle scallops curved along rich, elaborate quilting designs on the borders of Pansy Time and Blossom Time. A pieced petal border enhanced the flower theme for the May Day Flower Baskets. Pieced tulips connected by flowing bands of color reinforced the blowing stems and leaves of a tulips in baskets design (see figure 4). The tulip border was especially original and daring, and no doubt a challenge for the quilter to assemble and finish off. These new borders revealed a creative, artistic sense and embodied a useful marketing idea. Ver Mehren had always sold the straight strip borders as an optional, separate component of the quilt. Now he began showing the same complex pieced

Figure 4. Ver Mehren's Tulip quilt with embroidered blocks and separate pieced border.

borders on different quilts. In the case of the medallion format, standardized at 72 x 72 inches, all of the six-inch wide borders were interchangeable, and made the completed quilt measure 84 x 84 inches.

Ver Mehren added some new, fairly simple block designs to update the later catalogs. He called the popular rosettes of hexagons Martha Washington's Rose Garden. A pieced butterfly looked very contemporary. Some of the added patterns had been in *Capper's Weekly* in the late 1920s. The fact that the illustrations were exactly the same could lead to the assumption that Ver Mehren either produced the Capper patterns or simply copied the pictures. Possibly, however, he hired the illustrator who had done the Capper drawings to depict some of the common designs for him. With the rapid output of catalogs in 1932 and 1933, plus the many pictures that were appearing in newspapers at the same time, he needed professional help with the art work.[39]

"Ready Cut Quilts," that is, kits with die-cut fabric pieces, enhanced the product line that Ver Mehren had to sell. He did not make this type of kit but may have ordered the ten designs from, or had them cut by, the Colonial Readicut Quilt Block Company of Kansas City, the forerunner of The Colonial Pattern Company, better known as Aunt Martha.[40]

Finally, Ver Mehren's catalogs included several pages of his quilting designs sold either on paper to trace or as perforated patterns to be used with stamping powder. The customer could also order "albums" or collections of full-size quilting patterns that suggested which designs to use with different pieced patterns. A "Quilting Album" of fifty designs cost thirty-five cents. A larger collection in the "Master Quilting Album" sold for fifty cents.

Ver Mehren's Catalogs: Distribution

The rapid production of catalogs in 1932 coincided with a wider distribution of Ver Mehren's products. *Capper's Weekly* of Topeka, Kansas, several other Capper-published magazines, and *The Royal Neighbor* of Rock Island, Illinois, were among the first to offer mostly the tried and true good sellers in the stamped goods line to new audiences.[41] In November 1932, and again in March 1933, *Successful Farming*, another Des Moines magazine with a circulation over one million, used several quilt patterns in feature-length articles and offered "*Successful Farming's* book of prize-winning colonial quilts and decorative needlework."[42] All of these publications directed orders and payments be sent to their own addresses.

Ver Mehren changed the covers of his catalogs so that each distributor would appear to be the actual provider of the goods. Accustomed to having the same catalog pages bound with different covers for the two Button and Pleating Companies, VerMehren was already familiar with the technique. He went to great lengths to customize books for Gertrude May who sold needlework supplies at her "Art Studio" in St. Joseph, Missouri, and broadcast the "Old Quilter" radio program on station KFEQ. *Colonial Quilts* with Gertrude May's name printed on the outside of the front cover and inside the back cover contained an extra page for her photograph, a message to her "radio friends," a poem about "Sun Bonnet Sue" written by her mother, and her own order blank.[43] Most catalogs, however, had only the inside covers custom printed. Sometimes the distributor's name was printed or simply hand stamped only on the outside front cover, especially on the last *Hope Winslow* books.

Colonial Quilts version two, with a *Des Moines Register* imprint, coincided with the beginning of Ver Mehren's patterns in Iowa's major newspaper on November 20, 1932. The offer of a free pattern for the Star of Bethlehem (an alternate name for the Lone Star) with the purchase of the twenty-five cent catalog enticed readers to send in their orders to 707 Locust Street in Des Moines. This address was Iowa Button and Pleating's new location, only a few doors from *The Des Moines Register* at 715 Locust.[44]

Syndication of Patterns in Newspapers

The quilt patterns appeared in *The Des Moines Register* with the by-line "Bettina." This name had been used by two local residents for a series of Bettina cookbooks published from 1917 to 1924. Louise Bennett Weaver, a former high school domestic science teacher and editor of the *Register's* household page in the early 1920s, collaborated with Helen Cowles LeCron, a poet, writer, and member of the family that owned and published *The Des Moines Register*.[45] The Des Moines Register and Tribune Syndicate distributed a recipe and household hints column under the Bettina name to other publications.[46] Either woman might have been connected to the pattern feature. It is clear that "Bettina" was not a part of Hubert Ver Mehren's company.

Early in 1933, newspapers across the country began carrying the quilt feature from the *Des Moines Register* but without the Bettina name.[47] It included a drawing of the design, promotional commentary, and directions for order-ing. The boldly illustrated layouts portrayed traditional and popular patterns, as well as dazzling new and difficult design concepts. In the large central medallion format, designs such as The Eastern Star, Giant Dahlia, Glorious Chrysanthemum, Royal Aster, Russian Sunflower, and the Sirius Star required complex pieces and often had sixteen seams meeting together at the mid-point. Intricate borders repeated design elements from the central motifs, edging the quilt with sharp points or small curves. Although the description of Golden Dahlia touted it as "a modern design for the woman of today who wants to create a quilt that is new and different and will go down in quilt history as one of the new designs for 1933," the Giant Dahlia became the most widely copied of all of Ver Mehren's designs (see figure 5).[48] *Needlecraft* magazine and its associated catalog offered the pattern in 1935.[49] An entire book devoted to the pattern revived the design in 1983, and inexpensive imported Giant Dahlia quilts are now on the market.[50]

The quilts made up of repeating units also presented striking vi-

Figure 5. The Giant Dahlia in medallion format designed by Hubert Ver Mehren.

Herbert Ver Mehren/Home Art Studios

Figure 6. Interlacing Squares with repeating pieced units designed by Hubert Ver Mehren.

sual graphic layouts (see figure 6). They, too, required careful piecing and challenged even the expert quilter. Ver Mehren's inexperience with quiltmaking probably freed him to push the limits of the usual construction methods and exploit curves and angles. He based many of the patterns on geometric stars (Diamond Field Star, Glimmering Christmas Star, Milky Way Star) or curved flower petals (Easter Lily, Morning Glory, Painted Daisy). In others he combined the star form with a flower theme (Clematis, Cosmos, Poinsetta [sic], Rose Star, Star Bouquet). Stars and curves created his Golden Wedding Ring, a more complicated version of the Double Wedding Ring design in which six

123

pieced rings, not four, interlock around six pointed stars (see figure 7). The total number of Ver Mehren's quilt patterns at the end of the newspaper series approached three hundred.

No evidence has been found to indicate how Ver Mehren's quilt patterns were distributed to dozens of newspapers from 1933 through 1934. Although the Des Moines and Tribune Syndicate was probably the source, *Editor and Publisher* did not include quilt patterns among the features supplied from Des Moines. No other syndicate listed these patterns either, however.[51]

Most of the newspapers directed pattern orders to "Needleart Department" at 609 South Paulina Street in Chicago. Present research has not been able to determine anything about the Needleart Company at this Chicago address. Ver Mehren probably found some kind of set-up in Chicago to handle the distribution operation, perhaps as a way to distance his pattern business from the joint operation of the two Button and Pleating companies. Ver Mehren was involved, neverthe-

Figure 7. Golden Wedding Ring designed by Hubert Ver Mehren.

less, at least to the extent of corresponding with customers. When Lillian (Lillie) Carpenter ordered the kit for the center of a Rising Sun quilt, a typed response on Needleart Company letterhead dated April 13, 1933, was signed "HVM."[52]

Only the Paulina Street address and the mention of the *Colonial Quilts* book have connected the newspaper columns to Hubert Ver Mehren. Because pattern collectors found a Nancy Lee by-line on some of the columns and the same name at the bottom of the introductory page of *Colonial Quilts* version four, they assumed she was a Ver Mehren alias or associate and, therefore, everything associated with Nancy Lee was his work. More likely, however, this was a person connected to the Chicago operation who added products from other sources. A few items with the Nancy Lee by-line, especially the designs for nursery rhyme quilts, were very different from Ver Mehren's style. They came from a catalog called *The Needle Art Vogue Style Book D*, which also had the Paulina Street address on the cover and "Nancy Lee's" signature and photo inside.[53] The "Nancy Lee" Needleart Company syndicate was probably responsible for adding this material to the newspaper columns, and the only way to tell which is which is by analyzing styles or knowing the items from the different catalogs.

Home Art Studios

So far, no mention has been made of Home Art Studios, the title usually associated with the designs of Hubert Ver Mehren, because the name did not appear on his patterns until about 1934, several years after he started producing them. The Home Art Company or Home Art Studios had been in existence, however, since about 1930 under the proprietorship of "Mary Jacobs," the maiden name of Ver Mehren's wife (see figure 8). The Home Art Company was the couple's home-based, retail mail-order business.[54] In a textbook example of mail-order advertising technique, she used small classified magazine ads for a quilting attachment, then followed up the contact with a free premium offer in return for additional orders for quilting hoops, patterns, or materials.[55]

The very first *Colonial Quilts and Decorative Needlework* book was a catalog for the Home Art Company with Mary Jacobs' name on the cover. It presented a variety of goods assembled from several wholesale sources, among them Iowa Button & Pleating. Mary gave a home and family touch to the catalog. She pointed out that finished needlework items would be good sellers for "church societies, guild, ladies' aid and bazaars" and asked customers to "write for my special plans for church organizations." The Mary Jacobs cover of the color version of *Colonial Quilts and Decorative Needlework* (1931–1932) bore the new business title, "Home Art Studios."

Although Mary Jacobs was listed as the proprietor of Home Art Studios, she and her husband worked closely together to develop their own enterprise separate from the Ver Mehren family's Button and Pleating operations. As the pattern business flourished, he moved the catalogs away from the Pleating company and identified himself with the products of his own creation. Ver Mehren copyrighted the 1933 publications under his name and a year later changed the quilt patterns from Iowa Button and Pleating wholesale products to also being Home Art Studios retail items. The first appearance of the Home Art Studios name printed on the pattern sheets occurred next to a 1934 copyright date.[56]

During this same time period, in addition to juggling the two businesses, designing many new patterns for the newspapers, and dealing with rising costs as indicated by hand-stamped notices of price increases in some of the catalogs, Ver Mehren was also taking care of his wife and children. Mary had become ill with cancer in 1931. Trips to the Mayo Clinic for treatments were followed by periods of convalescence. Even while she was at the Rochester, Minnesota, hospital, Mary continued to help with bookkeeping as she did at home. They could not get domestic help because people feared cancer was contagious, so Hubert managed the household himself. Mary died at age 53 in 1937.[57]

The syndicated newspaper feature disappeared by the end of 1934, but it had provided quilters with patterns just when they were learning about the Sears quilt contest for the 1933 Chicago World's Fair. Encouraged by the many cash prizes, quilters quickly accepted the challenge of stitching Ver Mehren's spectacular layouts, and several received top awards. Lillie Belle Shaffer Carpenter won the Philadelphia regional semifinals with "a show-stopping design," an orange and

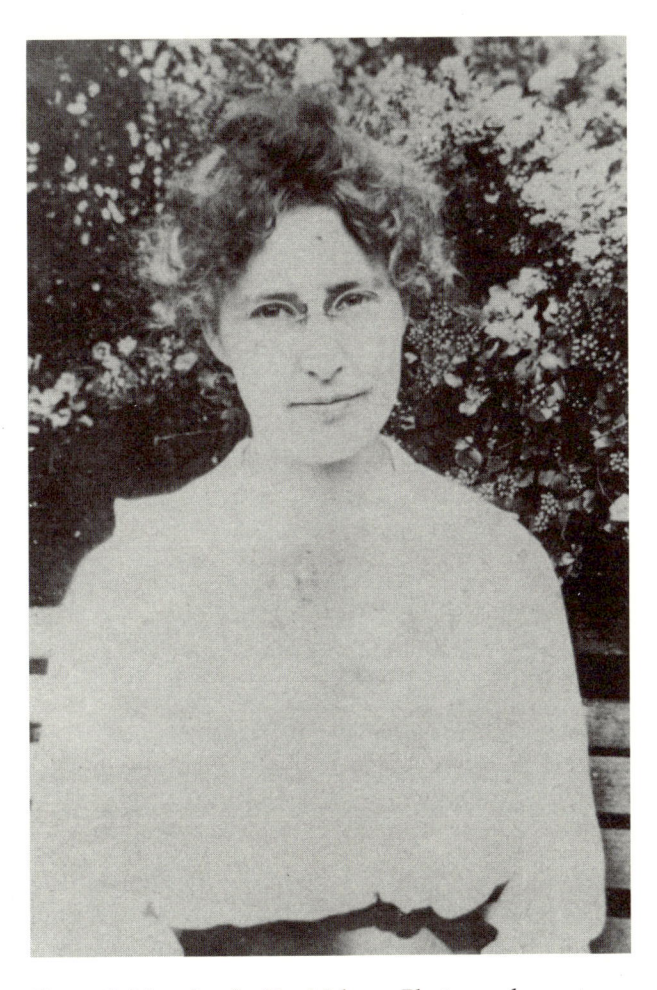

Figure 8. Mary Jacobs Ver Mehren. Photograph courtesy of Mary VerMehren Fowler.

yellow Sunburst made from a Ver Mehren stamped kit. Susie Combs was first in the Atlanta Region with the Star of France design. Both quilts were part of the display of regional winners at the Century of Progress Exposition in 1934.[58] Another Sunburst quilt made by Helen Downs later demonstrated the pattern's continuing appeal when *Good Housekeeping* chose it as the Indiana winner in the 1977 Great Quilt Contest.[59]

Through the rest of the decade of the 1930s, Ver Mehren supplied some patterns for occasional ads and features in *Wallaces' Farmer* (23 November 1935), *Successful Farming* (December 1939), and the *Farmers Market Bulletin* in Des Moines, and in *Needlecraft* (July 1935) and *Rural Progress* (November 1935), magazines beyond the borders of Iowa. In March 1936, *The Farmer's Wife* magazine from St. Paul, Minnesota, featured a new design with triangles that created the appearance of concentric hexagons called A Trip to Egypt, available as a pattern or stamped on three grades of cloth.[60] In 1940, Ver Mehren copyrighted his Bible History Quilt made up of thirty-five very detailed embroidered blocks and fifty-two squares quilted with a cross and crown. He took great care with the placement of the incidents from the Old and New Testaments, the arrangement of the incidents in the life of Jesus into a central cross, and the selection of ecclesiastical colors. At the end of the instructions he added: "Our daily lives are influenced by our surroundings. What greater inspiration could we have than to have this pictorial story of the Life of Christ on the Cross as our daily reminder. Making this beautiful quilt will be an unforgettable period in your life."[61]

The pattern business declined to almost nothing in the 1940s, although Ver Mehren kept his remaining inventory. The Iowa Button and Pleating Company continued to offer such services as stitching monograms, embroidering jackets, and making pennants and flags for colleges and clubs. Ver Mehren usually bought United States flags from outside manufacturers, but when they guessed wrong about the arrangement of the stars after Alaska became the forty-ninth state in 1958, he designed and made the new flag to sell (see figure 9).[62]

In the early 1950s the textile painting hobby of his secretary led Ver Mehren to design some stencils, sell supplies, and produce a catalog for the craft under the Home Art Studios label. The secretary, Marie Towle, lent her actual name to the marketing of the products . As part of her Pen Pal Club she offered a choice of a free painting board, painting tray, or brush to anyone who would send in five postcards pre-addressed to friends who might be interested in fabric painting. The phenomenal 25 percent response to this marketing promotion earned Ver Mehren recognition in *Advertising Age* magazine.[63]

In 1964–1965 Ver Mehren tried to revive a few favorite medallions for the *Jay Bees* and *Little 'N Big* magazines. When there were delays in

NEW FLAG DESIGN

Hubert Ver Mehren, Des Moines flag maker, works over a United States flag he is making to illustrate the new 49-star design.

Figure 9. Newspaper clipping, circa June 1958, courtesy of Dick Ver Mehren.

filling orders for the Giant Dahlia, he wrote to the readers about the difficulties in getting the old patterns re-made and commented:

> Lots of people tell me that I am working too long and so forth, but if you are happy in what you are doing, and the people that use the patterns get

pleasure and enjoyment from the patterns, I get the same satisfaction from making the pattern, gives the art that I seem to have been blessed with a chance to express itself.[64]

He also announced there would be six new medallion designs coming in future issues. Two of them, Carol's Delight, named for his granddaughter, and Glorious Rising Sun appeared in *JayBees Magazine* in November 1964. Continuing problems with unfilled orders caused an end to the pattern offers a year later.[65]

Ver Mehren continued to operate the Iowa Button and Pleating Company into his seventy-ninth year. On January 5, 1972, he was overcome by carbon monoxide from a defective chimney in his third-floor apartment above the business at 4301 Hubbell Avenue.[66] The city condemned and bulldozed the building and all its contents. Years earlier, fire in a storage building had destroyed the quilts that he used as display samples when he sold his patterns at the state fair.[67]

Conclusion

So, who was Hope Winslow? The photograph of the person on page one of *Hope Winslow's Quilt Book* gives her more substance than the other women encountered only as a name (see figure 10). The attractive young woman in the picture was probably Mary Ver Mehren's younger sister, Lutie, who lived in Omaha.[68] In spite of her realistic presence, Hope Winslow is the most fictitious character of all. Nothing indicates that Lutie had any actual role in the business. The personna of Hope Winslow was created to appeal to the customers of the Iowa Button and Pleating Company and Home Art Studios.

The research has uncovered information about the people whose names have been better known than Hubert Ver Mehren. Nancy Lee remains the most obscure, and more information about her would be very enlightening. One woman whose name has never been mentioned in connection with Home Art Studios may have had the most significant role in Ver Mehren's work and deserves more attention. Carlie Sexton wrote for the *Briardale Store News*. Did she influence Ver Mehren's production of stamped patterns, especially the Lone Star in four shades of one color? Was she responsible, therefore, for starting Ver

Figure 10. Mary Ver Mehren's younger sister, Lutie, was probably the model for this picture of "Hope Winslow" in *Hope Winslow's Quilt Book*.

Mehren on the path of designing his original medallion and pieced quilts? Even if the sequence did start with Carlie Sexton, Hubert Ver Mehren's own artistic ability carried him forward to create these unique twentieth-century patterns.

Ver Mehren's commitment to hard work and his mastery of marketing and mail-order merchandising probably exceeded his talent as an artist. These attributes enabled him to produce a popular line of goods, sell to various retail outlets, test new items, and keep old customers coming back with new orders. He tried to please the customers, arranged for individualized catalogs, and set up seemingly endless combinations of price and product options for buyers. Unfortunately, circumstances beyond his control beset him just at the high point of his endeavors, which, coincidentally, occurred at the time of the 1933 Sears Quilt Contest. His wife's health, the deepening Depression, and perhaps some problems inherent in the many ways patterns were ordered brought an end to the national exposure. Also, many of his patterns may have intimidated the average quilter, for even though they were drafted accurately, they required an expert with a needle to assemble the complicated shapes. These original designs were fifty years ahead of their time. Then with the decline in quiltmaking in the 1940s and 1950s, his pattern business eventually faded away.

Ver Mehren's contributions were never fully recognized. The Iowa Button and Pleating Company was primarily a service and wholesale operation where the proprietor did not identify himself with the products. About eight years after beginning to stamp goods for embroidery at Iowa Button and Pleating, Ver Mehren did begin to label his quilt patterns with the Home Art Studios name. Although he used female names and personae as marketing tools throughout his career, it is significant that he did not use such a device for his patterns, as some other companies did. Instead, he chose the business name associated with his wife. The Home Art Studios label should bring to mind the contributions of Mary Jacobs Ver Mehren as well as the achievements of her husband. But just as Marie Webster's designs are known by her name and not by the "Practical Patchwork" title of her pattern company, Hubert Ver Mehren's name should now be added to his patterns. I believe the best way of giving proper credit is to continue with the words "Home Art Studios" but *precede* them with the name of the man who added some amazing, original designs to our quiltmaking tradition. The designation should be: Hubert Ver Mehren/Home Art Studios.

Notes and References

1. For a discussion of the Colonial Revival in connection with quilts and patterns, see Jeanette Lasansky, "The Colonial Revival," *Pieced by Mother*, ed. Jeanette Lasansky (Lewisburg, PA: Oral Traditions Project, 1987), 104–15.

2. For more information about the proliferation of quilt-pattern companies in the early twentieth century, see Merikay Waldvogel, "Quilt Design Explosion of the Great Depression," *On the Cutting Edge*, ed. Jeannette Lasansky (Lewisburg, PA: Oral Traditions Project, 1994), 84–95.

3. Cuesta Benberry, letter to author, 19 September 1997, and lecture "Major Influences on the 20th Century Quilt Scene" at the 20th Century Quilts, 1900–1970: Women Make Their Mark Symposium, Paducah, KY, 28 June 1997.

4. Merikay Waldvogel kindly loaned a portion of Mildred Dickerson's Home Art Studios material for examination by the author.

5. U.S. Census for Iowa, 1900; Mary Ver Mehren Fowler, letter to author, 10 June 1997. Ver Mehren's daughter and son have graciously shared family information in letters, telephone calls, and interviews.

6. Mary Ver Mehren Fowler, interview with author, 11 July 1997.

7. Ibid., also telephone conversations with author, 1 November and 23 November 1999.

8. Although both Button and Pleating companies used "Inc." after their names and listed officers, neither Nebraska nor Iowa has any record of official incorporation.

9. *Des Moines City Directory*, 1922.

10. *Style Book of Iowa Button & Plaiting Co., Inc.* (Des Moines, IA: n.d.), author's collection; *Style Book of Ideal Button & Plaiting Co., Inc.* (Omaha, NE: n.d.), collection of Shirley McElderry.

11. Ibid., 72.

12. Mary Fowler remembers first being at the State Fair at the age of three when her brother was born. Both children recall helping their father at the fair in the 1930s. Quilts made from his patterns were on display in his booth. Fowler, 23 November 1999; Dick Ver Mehren, telephone conversation with author, 23 May 1997.

13. "Des Moines One of 6 Publishing Centers in U.S.," *Des Moines Tribune*, 28 November 1927.

14. Susan Price Miller, "Carlie Sexton and Her Quilt Pattern Business," *Uncoverings 1996*, ed.Virginia Gunn (San Francisco: American Quilt Study Group, 1996), 33–35.

15. Lucretia was Kathern's middle name, and King came from her mother's maiden name. Kathern married Carlton Chase Proper, Jr., who sold advertising for his father's *People's Popular Monthly*. After they left Iowa for California, she contributed free-lance articles to several magazines, including many for Caroline B. King at *Country Gentleman*. Kathern Ayres Proper, telephone interview with author, 29 October 1999.

16. Lucretia King, "February Fancy Work," *People's Popular Monthly*, February 1928, 19.

17. Kathern Ayres Proper, telephone interview with author, 7 November 1999.

18. Proper, 29 October and 7 November 1999.

19. Mary Fowler, 23 May and 11 July 1997.

20. "Mother's Old Fashioned Flower Garden Quilt Color Chart," (Omaha: Ideal Button & Pleating Co., 1931); collection of Wilene Smith. A flyer, "Colorful Cross Stitch Quilt Blocks" (Omaha: Ideal Button and Pleating Co., n.d.), in the collection of Wilene Smith, further illustrates the connection between the two businesses.

21. Proper, 7 November 1999.

22. *People's Popular Monthly*, January 1930, p. 30. A one-page flyer offered the premiums either free or at reduced cost with various subscription totals. Collection of Wilene Smith.

23. Proper, 7 November 1999.

24. Clipping from the Collection of Mildred Dickerson owned by Merikay Waldvogel. Kathern Ayres Proper supplied the date. The magazine company defaulted on loan payments and was bankrupt. "Proper Named Firm Receiver," *Des Moines Tribune*, 18 May 1931.

25. Yankee Pride pattern from the Collection of Mildred Dickerson owned by MerikayWaldvogel.

26. Four-page flyer with a return address for Lucretia King at Wilton Junction, Iowa, courtesy of Teddy Pruett and Shirley McElderry. Kathern Ayres Proper bought the goods at wholesale prices and sold them retail.

27. [Carlie Sexton] "Quaint Old Fashioned Quilts," *Briardale Store News*, November 1930, courtesy of Shirley McElderry; Carlie Sexton, *Old-Fashioned Quilts* (Wheaton, IL: by the author, 1928), 7.

28. For more information about Carlie Sexton, see Miller, 29–62.

29. Envelope and pattern of the Sunburst Design [Lone Star] with the number 25, indicating a production date of about 1930 or 1931 when Ver Mehren first started printing patterns for pieced designs. Collection of Shirley McElderry.

30. Color flyer from Younker Brothers, author's collection, thanks to Shirley McElderry.

31. Carol Dean, "Briardale Brings You These Feminine Keepsakes of American Traditions," *Briardale Store News*, September 1931, 3, courtesy of Cuesta Benberry. The first available example of the actual book offer documenting the title as *Briardale's Book of Colonial Quilts and Decorative Needlework* is from January 1932, courtesy of Shirley McElderry. The September 1932 issue advertised the next version of the catalog with the shortened title of *Colonial Quilts*, author's collection.

32. The author has a collection of nine books. Other examples and photocopies have been loaned by Shirley McElderry, Xenia Cord, Carolyn Miller, and by Merikay Waldvogel from her personal collection and her Collection of Mildred Dickerson, making a total of eighteen books and covers examined for this paper.

33. *Mary Jacob's Book of Colonial Quilts and Decorative Needle Work* (Des Moines: Home Art Co., ca. 1930), author's collection. The date is based on the series of

quilt patterns shown in consecutive numerical order from which the Briardale patterns were selected, beginning in the fall of 1930.

34. In addition to the *Briardale Store News*, an early notice appeared in the *Pennsylvania Farmer*, February 1932.

35. 1932 was the 200th anniversary of the birth of George Washington.

36. More variations may exist. A comparison of two copies of *Gertrude May's Book of Colonial Quilts* revealed different patterns in the bottom right corner of page 7. Author's collection and the Collection of Mildred Dickerson owned by Merikay Waldvogel.

37. *Mary Jacob's Book of Colonial Quilts and Decorative Needle Work*, 1.

38. Carlie Sexton, *Old-Time Patchwork Quilts* (Des Moines, IA: Successful Farming Publishing Co., ca. 1923), 16.

39. Some of Ver Mehren's later original designs appear to have been styled in the same manner as the Capper illustrations.

40. For the history of the companies of Jack and Clara Tillotson, see Barbara Brackman, "Mid-western Pattern Sources," in *Uncoverings 1980*, ed. Sally Garoutte (Mill Valley, CA: American Quilt Study Group, 1980) 7–10. Colonial inaugurated their long-running series of needlework pages in *The Royal Neighbor* with five "Ready Cut Quilt Blocks for Quilts and Pillows" in October 1930. Ruby McKim also offered Ready Cut kits in *The Royal Neighbor* beginning in January 1931. Carol Beeding, head of public relations for Royal Neighbors of America, a fraternal life insurance company in Rock Island, IL, graciously copied all needlework material from the monthy magazines between 1926 and 1935 for this research.

41. Microfilms of *Capper's Weekly* and the Capper-owned *Pennsylvania Farmer* were surveyed from the late 1920s to the mid-1930s. Through the resourcefulness of Linda Glendening, the Pella, Iowa, public library obtained reels of microfilm and other materials through interlibrary loan. Her interest and help kept this research going forward and are much appreciated.

42. *Successful Farming*, November 1932, 9.

43. *Gertrude May's Book of Colonial Quilts*, author's collection.

44. *Des Moines City Directory*, 1934.

45. Annual entries in the *Des Moines City Directory* chronicle Louise B. Weaver's employment. Helen Cowles LeCron, "Other Writers of Promise and Fulfillment," *A Book of Iowa Authors by Iowa Authors*, Johnson Brigham, ed. (Des Moines, IA: Iowa State Teachers Association, 1930) [235]. The cookbooks featured recipes interwoven with narratives about Bettina and her husband, family and friends, as well as poems to introduce each section.

46. "Annual Directory of Syndicate Features," *Editor and Publisher*, 5 June 1926.

47. Beginning dates: January 22 in the *Wheeling News*, courtesy of Zoe Smith; January 24 in the *Fort Wayne Journal-Gazette*; February 20 in the *Wichita Beacon* and *Kansas City Star*, cited in Wilene Smith, *Home Art Studios. Time Line and Reference List*, ©September 22, 1995; March 13 in the *Columbus Dispatch*. Edna Paris Ford in "Those Beautiful Home Art Studio [sic] Quilt Patterns," *Quilt World Omnibook*, Spring, 1981, 10, reported the patterns were in "at least 96 newspapers and magazines throughout the country."

48. Golden Dahlia description from *Hope Winslow's Quilt Book* (Des Moines, IA: H. Ver Mehren, 1933), 2.

49. *Needlecraft, The Home Arts Magazine,* July 1935, 24; *Needlecraft . . . Book of Materials* (catalog), ca. 1935, author's collection.

50. Susan Aylsworth Murwin and Suzzy Chalfant Payne, *The Quick and Easy Giant Dahlia Quilt* (New York: Dover Publications, Inc: 1983); ad for $39.99 "Green Dahlia" quilt at Younkers Department Store, Des Moines, IA, August 1997, author's collection.

51. *Editor and Publisher* included an "Annual Directory of [Syndicate] Features" in one issue each year. The years 1926, 1927, 1930–1934 were examined.

52. Letter courtesy of Merikay Waldvogel. The letterhead of the Needleart Company stated that it was "Not Inc."

53. *The Needle Art Vogue Style Book D* (Chicago: Needleart Co., n.d.), courtesy of Cuesta Benberry.

54. Fowler, 10 June 1997.

55. Ad, *Better Homes & Gardens,* February 1935, 62, courtesy of Shirley McElderry. Flyer from Home Art Co., n.d., signed by Mary Jacobs, courtesy of Wilene Smith.

56. "The Gorgeous Chrysanthemum Quilt," printed with the words "Copyright 1934 Home Art Studios Des Moines Iowa" in an envelope with a *Des Moines Register* clipping of the pattern dated 11 March 1934, collection of Shirley McElderry.

57. Mary Fowler, 23 May 1997. Mary remembers her father with great admiration: "He was quite a guy, fair, and believed in hard work." Fowler, 23 November 1999.

58. Merikay Waldvogel and Barbara Brackman, *Patchwork Souvenirs of the 1933 World's Fair* (Nashville: Rutledge Hill Press, 1993), 39–42, 57, 97.

59. "51 Prize-Winning Quilts," *Good Housekeeping,* March 1978, 128.

60. Original pattern of A Trip to Egypt copyrighted 1936, courtesy of Shirley McElderry.

61. Original pattern of the Bible History Quilt, author's collection.

62. "A Pattern For New U.S. Flag," newspaper clipping, ca. June 1958, courtesy of Dick Ver Mehren.

63. Ver Mehren, 23 May 1997.

64. "A letter from Van. . . . " in the column "An Old-Fashioned Quilting Party," Claudine Moffatt, *Jay Bees Magazine,* September 1964, n.p., courtesy of Cuesta Benberry.

65. [Claudine Moffatt], *Jay Bees Magazine,* November 1965, n.p., courtesy of Cuesta Benberry.

66. Hubert Ver Mehren obituary, *Des Moines Tribune,* 7 January 1972, 9.

67. Ver Mehren, 23 May 1997; Fowler, 23 May 1997.

68. Fowler, 10 June 1997. Mary knows nothing about "Hope Winslow" but she believes the picture is of her Aunt Lutie.

"Petting the Fabric": Medium and the Creative Process

Lisa Gabbert

The sensory aspects of fabric, particularly its color, hand, and the ways in which it is used are aspects of the creative process in quilting that deserve greater scholarly attention. Emphasizing the sensory rather than the philosophical meanings of the term "aesthetic," this paper looks at the relationship between creativity, sensory experience, and artistic medium in a group of quilters in central Idaho. Drawing primarily on the words of the quilters themselves, this research suggests that the look, hand, and particular way of manipulating fabric in quilting are key creative stimuli. This study also suggests that the relationship and response of the artist to her/his chosen material constitutes a basic dynamic without which creativity cannot emerge and art cannot be produced.

The sensory aspects of fabric are an important part of quilting that have been neglected in quilting scholarship. This study demonstrates that fabric evoked a basic, positive aesthetic response in the quilters who participated in this study. In doing so, it provided a key source of artistic inspiration that the quilters did not find in other media and therefore played a primary role in their creative processes. Furthermore, the particular way in which fabric is cut up, arranged, and sewn back together in quilting also provided creative stimulus, suggesting that both the material itself and the ways in which it is used play an integral role in motivating people to create textile art.

In examining aesthetic choice and artistic inspiration, most quilting scholars have adhered to contemporary conceptions that involve either notions of taste or an articulated set of prescribed rules, a perspective that has led few researchers to attend to the importance of fabric itself in the creative process for people who quilt. John Forrest reminded us, however, that notions of aesthetics also invoke sensory experiences that should be taken into account.[1] Researchers such as Sharon Sherman and Linda Pershing have also pointed out the influence of the senses as important aspects of aesthetic experience and creativity.[2] This perspective is compatible with a growing interest in phenomenological methodologies, sometimes defined as the description of experience as told and lived by informants.[3]

Forrest suggested that a more complete ethnography of aesthetic objects and aesthetic evaluation involves a full description of sensory experience, including taste, touch, smell, and sound as well as sight. This approach poses obvious ethnographic difficulties. An emphasis on sensory experience, however, is useful for understanding the experience of the individual, which can provide insights into how and why people create art. At least in this case study, an initial examination of sensory experience led to a closer examination of the role the particular medium played in art and creativity. In this study I used the quilters' descriptions of their own sensory experience and their statements about their relationship to their medium of choice as evidence that fabric evokes a positive aesthetic response that is a fundamental aspect of quilting. Results suggest that the medium with which artists work is a primary source of inspiration and creativity for them. I examined the importance of fabric as a creative stimulus from both a group and an individual perspective and postulate that not only is the relationship between maker and medium essential to the creative process, but also that only after they "found their medium" were many quilters in the group examined able to define themselves as artists.

The Pine Needle Quilters

Influenced by the fine scholarship of Joyce Ice, my initial approach to this fieldwork was to further explore the interpersonal relations among women as a function of the quilting group.[4] I worked with the Pine Needle Quilters in McCall, Idaho, a small town located in the central portion of the state. At the time, the group consisted of about twenty-two female members, approximately ten to fourteen of whom attended regularly. My mother is a member and brought me to my first meeting where I was welcomed. The quilters, who ranged in age from the mid-thirties through the late seventies, were conversing about the menopausal changes women experience as they enter late middle age. "I heard one guy describing this place as a stitch and bitch club!" Joyce McFadden gleefully exclaimed. "Hoo-boy, it's hot in here." She fanned herself vigorously despite the chilly March temperature, while several other women nodded sympathetically. A few minutes later, as the women gathered around the table to begin their business meeting, an older member demonstrated the ease with which a rubber latex thimble could push a needle through fabric. The others jumped on the opportunity to allude to the thimble's other potential uses as she waggled it suggestively on her thumb. I was delighted to have found this diverse and rather bawdy group of women.

My research was straightforward. At the second meeting I asked the Pine Needles members permission to conduct fieldwork. "Yeah Yeah! Study us!" was their unified response. I observed only; it should be noted that there was no quilting frame up while I attended the weekly meetings.[5] Instead, members brought in their own projects to work on or simply for "show-and-tell." I also conducted interviews with six women who were considered some of the "core" members of the group since they attended every week. Their background and quilting perspectives varied greatly. The youngest quilter was in her early forties and the eldest was in her seventies. Members of the group I interviewed made both bed quilts and wall hangings, quilted by both hand and by machine, and ranged widely in socioeconomic background.

As I observed the group and interviewed the quilters, their passion for quilting and love of fabric quickly became apparent, permeating the other aspects of quilting to which my studies had me attuned. Some scholars have suggested that women form groups because they share a common interest in quilting.[6] While an interest in quilting is obviously necessary for participation, it was not the primary reason for joining the quilting group among the Pine Needles. Rather, for the people I interviewed, the initial impetus to join seemed to be only a moderate interest in quilting and more prominently a desire for company—along with an intimacy with fabric as a medium. This desire for companionship, rather than a direct interest in quilting, has been noted by Susan Stewart and others.[7] Yet while this was true for many members of the Pine Needles, it was their familiarity with fabric that allowed that social interaction to occur. Several informants, for example, had perhaps attempted to make one quilt on their own and had then set quilting aside until they became members of the group. Leta Polivka recalled, "The winters are really long here and I needed some companionship." She had quilted a pillow from a kit before joining the group, but stated "I don't think that I would have gotten as interested as fast as I did if I hadn't found the club."[8] Jackie Zbrowski joined the club because of a friend and said, "There was probably about three or four months during which I went to the group and until I started quilting. . . . it looked like a jigsaw puzzle to me at first, like 'How in the world?' It was just beyond me. But little by little I just did it."[9] For these women then, while the initial impetus to join the group was social, their background in sewing and experience with fabric allowed them to learn and participate. Catherine Petzak commented, "Of course I've always liked fabric—I've always sewn garments and curtains and you know, whatever you need. I think that's maybe what got me started."[10]

Pat Ferrero, Elaine Hedges, and Julie Silber identified sewing as a common denominator for women who quilt, but did not mention the unifying element of fabric.[11] Doris Dyen noted in her own research among quilters that "Most of the women had prior experience with needlework before joining the Quiltmakers, but usually it was with undecorated, functional sewing, such as making and mending clothes or curtains."[12] This was true among the Pine Needles. All of them had sewn all their lives and were intimately familiar with working with needles. But familiarity with fabric as a potentially artistic medium is another element of this common denominator that is often overlooked. Karen Burton was a seamstress before she joined, and Billie Hawley, who has sewn all her life, told me, "I had a visual memory of me once, born with a needle in my hand."[13] Leta said that her background in sewing "[is] very handy now, a lot of the things in the past that I have done have really helped me now [with quilting]."[14]

Fabric as Source of Artistic Inspiration

"I don't care about anything but quilting," Jackie once told me, and from what I observed, the Pine Needles were certainly crazy about quilting. Nearly all of my informants stated that once they discovered quilting, they knew that they had found what they were "meant to do." Karen Burton noted, "It was just like love at first sight. I can't live without this and now there aren't enough hours in the day. I just discovered that I had a passion for it, and of course the other ladies did too."[15]

Jane Przybysz has pointed out that quilters often characterize their craze for quilting as an "addiction," (there is a tongue-in-cheek list of traits that determines whether one qualifies for Fabriholics Anonymous). For the Pine Needles, this love extended to other material forms. During the meetings I saw women reading books like *Murder at the Quilt Show*. They organized quilting retreats and bought cookbooks called *Favorite Recipes of Quilters* as well as quilting calendars and t-shirts. Przybysz suggested that this addiction to quilting is the "female desire to materially and symbolically amplify and extend the self." Women who quilt, for example, often take over whole rooms of the house (and often parts of the yard) with their activity.[16] Przybysz proposed a direct relationship between quilting and the body and her suggestion potentially accounts for a psychological satisfaction derived from quilting. Her perspective, however, does not address why quilters crave quilting as opposed to other art forms. When I asked my informants why quilters were so crazy about quilting, their answers suggested first that the fabric itself constituted an extremely important factor because of its particular sensory qualities and second, that quilting as a particular kind of act allowed them to use fabric in a way that was aesthetically satisfying. For them, working with fabric was something quite different from other activities. It allowed them to create in ways that other media did not. Catherine stated, "And of course once you start, it's just wonderful. It's hard to stop."[17]

One of the primary underlying sources of inspiration for most Pine Needle members was the integral relationship between fabric and color. The importance of color has been pointed out numerous times. Yvonne Milspaw, for example, noted that quilter Jennie Bedient's strong sense of color was an integral part of her overall design.[18] But the specific connection between color and fabric as a conveyor of color is often left implicit. For many quilters in the Pine Needles, color and fabric were inexorably interconnected in the same sentence, and many identified their love of color as stemming from childhood experiences with cloth. Jackie recalled that as a girl, her mother would take her to the store to buy fabric:

> And it used to be, a man stood behind the counter and then the rolls were up and you had to choose from behind, you could not touch it. So, I remember looking at all the beautiful colors. And I've been sort of hooked on colors ever since.[19]

Emily Ede also said her favorite thing in the world is color:

> And I love color and I love fabric. I've always loved fabric too. My mother loved fabric and she always bought fabric. She had a lot of our clothes made. And we always had fabric scraps and I always used to sew them, wrap them around my dolls. I started making doll clothes, so I always had lots of fabric scraps to play in. And it's fun to play with the color, the different prints, and the textures.[20]

To Billie, "Primarily the fabric comes first. Or the colors. *I* would say. I have an idea of what colors. To me, the fabric just always finds me right away. I think I'm lucky in that I work well with color."[21] Karen's favorite part of quilting is picking out the fabric, while Catherine commented, "I think color probably catches my eye first. If I see a quilt in colors that I don't particularly like then I'm apt to skip over it more quickly than I would if it was colors that I really really liked—that were pleasing to me."[22]

Furthermore, colors seemed intricately associated with the fabric's more tactile aspects. Touch was an important tool of aesthetic evaluation. Called the "fabric hand" in textile scholarship, this sensory experience entails how fabrics feel when touched or held. Textile scholars have long recognized the importance of the hand in determining a textile's aesthetic qualities and understand the difficulty in measuring this important mode of evaluation.[23] Because the quilters stressed the fabric hand in a number of ways, it seemed important as a source of artistic inspiration. In conversation, for example, Jackie moved from the subject of color variation to the tactile differences between washed and unwashed cottons in the same thought: "I like the material. The feel of the material and the different variations of your light, dark, medium shades. I think that's kind of fun." When asked to explain further, Jackie commented:

> Well, I want to make sure that the cloth is always a good texture and weave. All cotton. And that it washes. I always wash them and dry them and iron them again before I ever use them in case there is any shrinkage. But I also don't like that sizing in it. Now some people do keep it in, especially wall hangings, people who do wall hangings instead of quilts. Course, it's never going to be washed. And they like that slickness. But I don't. So, that's part of it.[24]

Karen also thought touch was important. She mentioned that she just liked the feel of the cotton in general: "Cause you can run the fabric through your fingers, you know. It's a very kinesthetic thing—I mean when I was little I would run my sheets between my fingers. There's a feel to it, I think. Especially cottons and things, the coolness of the fabric. It's a whole kinesthetic, sensual experience."[25] Billie and Catherine also liked the feel of fabric. Billie said that the whole sensation of touch was very important to her, while Catherine stated, "I love working with the fabric. Your mother has accused me more than once of petting the fabric. *Love* the feel of it."[26] Leta, on the other hand, did not particularly like the feel of flat cottons, but her favorite part of quilting was the actual handwork itself because it transformed a flat cotton surface into a textured one: "It's a relaxation time. And then the quilting—it's the texture. . . . you look back on it and it's totally different than the flat piece of fabric was when you started."[27] For Emily, the tactile aspects lay in the warmth of the final product:

> It's just—something about cloth and fabric. It's very—it's tactile and comforting. I always feel like I'm creating something that a lot of people will get a lot of enjoyment out of. That makes me feel good. And it's going to last after me. It's warmth and all that stuff. You can wrap up in it, and you can touch it, and a lot of art you can't touch.[28]

Thus, although the particularities of what each woman liked to touch and what each associated with the fabric hand differed, in each case these aspects seemed to be an essential stimulus in motivating her to create.

Apart from the look and hand, the acquisition of cloth was an important part of the quilters' lives. Collecting is a phenomenon that often inspires awe or puzzlement to outsiders. While the acquisition of fabric is not a sensory aspect of quilting, the feeling with which collectors pursue their object of desire is fervent. For the quilters, collecting fabric is of prime importance in their lives. The Pine Needles collected textiles passionately and many had shelves filled with fabric. Billie admitted that "I have enough fabric that if for some reason they stop producing fabric, I think I'll be OK."[29] During their vacations, spare time, and in-between work breaks, the quilters actively sought out fabric shops, often driving hundreds of miles to check out a sale or a new store. Often, they came to meetings with new fabrics for show-and-tell instead of an actual project.

The existing scholarship on collecting, however, rarely focuses on the collection of raw materials by people who actually use them and only very recently has begun to examine the collection of "non-art" objects.[30] Instead, much scholarship focuses on the psychological aspects of collecting, on the connoisseurship and taste of the collectors, or on the monetary value of the collection.[31] While fabric functioned as an object of consumption for the Pine Needles, the quilters harbored no illusion that their fabric collections would increase in value. Rather, they simply recognized that they often spent a good deal of money pursuing their interest. Joyce Ice noted that one of the church quilters with whom she worked once commented, "You should have asked us how much we spend on quiltmaking, not how much we make."[32] Indeed, a quilter's expenditures may seem extreme to other members of the family and spending this money is, perhaps, a way to maintain some power or a feeling of control.[33] Leta is not wealthy and said that when she ordered brown fabric to frame one quilt, "The idea that I would order fabric and pay ten dollars a yard for it seemed like a big deal."[34] Karen said that her husband has claimed more than once, "We could take a trip around the world on what you've spent on fabric."[35]

Yet collecting for the quilters seemed based in tactile, sensory, and emotional satisfaction rather than in issues of monetary control. Value lay in simply shopping for and acquiring their chosen medium. Jackie said, "If I go into a fabric store, it's just like looking at chocolate candy. I wish I could have all of it. But I can't have it all, so sometimes I just buy pieces of it."[36] Necessity and use were secondary issues. Catherine said that she keeps fabric for three or four years before she decides what to do with it and that each piece has a particular memory or association attached to it: "Most all of my fabric, even the fat quarters, I can tell you where I bought it and under what circumstances. It just indicates how interesting it is to me, that's all."[37] Karen said:

> I don't know what it is. I have shelves and shelves of fabric. More fabric than I could ever use in a lifetime if I started tomorrow and made one quilt a day... There is something to me, you know, that kinesthetic, that feel of fabric, that look, the color, looking at it stacked all together on the shelves, the fabric is just the most important thing. I don't even have to do anything with some of it, it can just sit there.

She continued, "I have to have one of every book and a yard of every fabric before I die. This is my goal in life."[38]

The Quilting Process

The cloth alone, however, does not explain why quilters quilt, and another aspect important to creative inspiration in quilting seems to be the physical act of manipulating fabric in a particular manner. The color, hand, and acquisition of fabric can be or are part of other forms of sewing, yet making clothes or curtains did not motivate or inspire the quilters in the same way. For many members, sewing was too rigid and did not allow for the flexible manipulation of colors and textures that is possible in quilting forms. Leta was simply so bored with sewing that she stopped when she was eighteen and did not pick it up again until she joined the Pine Needles. She said "I'd done everything and I was tired of it.... I didn't want to pursue it."[39] Jackie said quilting for her is different than sewing because "It [quilting] is just a lot of fun. You know. It's sort of intriguing. The more I do, the more I can't wait to do three or four ahead."[40]

Such comments suggest that the particular kind of action involved in quilting is essential, a fact noted by Sandra K. D. Stahl who wrote that "[a]nother important part of the process is the cutting and sewing of the pieces that make up the top of the quilt."[41] For many Pine Needles members, exhilaration lay in designing by this particular process. Leta, for example, stressed the importance of being able to manipulate color—that even when she worked with a color she did not like such as purple, she could control it by putting it next to brown to make it fade away instead of using yellow which "made it stick out like a sore thumb."[42] Billie said "Basically painting with fabric is what I try to do. It may not look like a painting, but you know, working fabric is a medium in which you put pictures together. We cut it up in little squares and triangles or whatever, and put it back together in something new. I like that process a lot." She later said, "I love cutting things up and putting them back together in a new way. That's the best way I can describe it."[43] Karen noted, "I think I've always liked fabric and I've always liked sewing. And I like the way it goes together and I don't know what it is. Put it together, you know, disparate pieces of fabric or something." Later in our conversation Karen elaborated on this aspect, stating that in quilting she can break rules: "We are brought up with rules, you know, you don't wear these colors together, or put these lines together. One of the first things I learned in quilting is that there are no rules."[44] In contrast, for Jackie the ultimate appeal of re-creation and reassembly lies not in breaking rules, but in the orderly precision of putting something back together. She said:

> [I]t is a whole new thing making a large blanket from tiny tiny pieces of cloth. And they have to be so precise, that if you are off by an eighth, and if you continue to do that, the quilt is ruined by the end because you would be off maybe two or three inches on one side. Or, they wouldn't fit together. And I find that interesting. I like it—I have to have it just right.[45]

Emily also liked the challenge of working with small pieces, although to her, being "off " did not necessarily mean the quilt was ruined: "And I really love quilting. I love the challenge of fitting the pieces together just right—don't always get them together just right, but if you don't get them together just right it's still beautiful."[46] Thus, while the reasons the quilters enjoyed cutting up cloth and putting it back together differed, this act was essential because the color and texture that inspired the women were enhanced by the particular mode of creation. Cutting up cloth and creating a new whole allowed for greater freedom and challenges than other forms of sewing and suggests that not only is the medium important, but that the way in which the medium is manipulated is essential for artistic creation and inspiration.

The Group as Source of Inspiration

With all the emphasis on fabric, I was curious why the quilting group was still important, since the quilters continued to attend the quilting meetings—often religiously—even after many of them had become extremely competent. What I found was that the group was essential to many members' development as artists because the group provided feedback about fabric and color control, and quilting in general. The Pine Needles met on Monday nights and if Christmas Eve fell on a Monday, I was told, some members would be quilting away at their meeting place in the local library. Catherine said that the only Monday night that she had missed in the past year was for her thirty-fifth wedding anniversary, although she thought that quilting on Christmas Eve was "a little extreme."

For many years researchers have pointed to the strong bonds that quilters develop and which play an important role in their lives, functioning as an outlet for psychological stress and tension and providing positive feedback and a sense of satisfaction among members.[47] Certainly personal relationships among the women were important to the Pine Needles. Catherine, for example, commented that she loved the age diversity and background: "I remember thinking, 'in this small group of people, in this tiny little town, McCall, Idaho, everything in the world that has happened, has happened to this group.'"[48] While the quilters formed important interpersonal relationships in the group, however, they emphatically stressed that an essential function was the sharing of artistic ideas.[49] Jackie commented, "You know, we learn from each other. The ideas, or ask questions, or if you have a problem, you can ask. So, that's why I go."[50] Leta agreed that going to the group was stimulating because, "Somebody was always exited about a new fabric or something."[51] Catherine said that she uses colors and techniques that she would never have tried on her own. "Of course, we talk about a lot of other things besides quilting. *But I love the medium which gets us there"* [emphasis mine].[52]

Catherine's statements fit well with my own observations. There was certainly a lot of socializing and bonding in the group, but the majority of talk was about quilting and quite often fabric in particular. Members shared a host of magazine articles and how-to books. They talked about patterns and colors and fabrics and who had what fabrics on sale and quilting tools and quilting techniques. At my second meeting, for example, the Pine Needles informed me that they had arranged for a speaker. When the "speaker" arrived, the quilters sat around the table and quieted down. The woman stood up, introduced herself, and without another word passed around yards of swirling multicolored fabrics that she had dyed by hand, most of which did not make it past the first couple of women before they were claimed as sold. The rest of the meeting was spent admiring the beautiful cloth by literally "petting the fabric." Each piece of fabric was passed from woman to woman; each woman unfolded it, stroked it, perhaps traced the pattern with a finger, refolded it, patted the bulk, and passed it along to the next person if she was not going to buy.

At the meetings, the women laughed and joked a lot about their husbands, kids, and the trials of being female, but serious and intimate conversations were rare, suggesting that while the women firmly believed they could come to the group for emotional support, they did not often do so explicitly. I heard only one troubled personal experience narrative during my ten weeks with them, which was ironically framed as a fabric shopping expedition. As the women joked one evening about the lucky ones who were not married, one member told how she had once stolen a credit card and run away from her husband, checked into a hotel in a nearby city, and went fabric shopping for three days without once calling home.

What emerged in many of the conversations with the quilters was the fact that the women often did not realize they were "artistic" until they began attending the group and learning to quilt. Along with the quilting process, the feedback from the group helped the women look at what they were doing as creative. Karen laughingly recalled that her children used to save her *Pictionary* drawings because they were so funny: "So I just thought, well, I'm not an artist."[53] Emily felt similarly:

> I didn't even realize that I was an artist. I always wanted to be an artist, but didn't realize that I was born an artist until I started going there [to the group].... They encouraged me and they liked what I did. They said, "you're so good with color." I didn't really realize that. I knew I liked my color combinations, but I didn't realize that other people might.[54]

Several women stated that they had tried more conventional forms of artistic expression such as painting and sculpture, but that nothing had "felt right" until they began quilting. Billie said that working with fabric felt more "natural" to her, while Catherine described herself as a very directed, rule-oriented person; painting intimidated her, but she felt she could let herself go with fabric in a way she could not with other media: "Maybe because it's that I'm more familiar with fabric than with other mediums, you know, I can do more, I'm freer to play with it than I am some of the other things."[55] Karen hypothesized that this was because "you can be an artist with fabric maybe where you can't with some of those other mediums."[56] Her comment suggests that people respond in different ways to different media, and that perhaps creativity happens only after an artist has found materials that for her/him are both appealing and technically manageable. As illustrated earlier, certainly these women were intimately familiar with and loved fabric. They found that the specific actions involved in quilting allowed them to explore creatively and they received positive feedback from the quilting group. They began to redefine themselves as artists. As Emily noted, "I just think I've found my medium."[57]

Conclusion

For many years, Alan Dundes, professor of folklore and anthropology at Berkeley, has called upon folklorists to interpret their data, to explain the why of folklore materials. Literally embracing a definition of aesthetics as sensory experience and listening closely to statements by informants about their medium of choice led to a closer examination of the role of the materials and physical processes that are integral to the creation of art. The answer to any "why" question is always complex. Certainly there are many other facets that inform the quilters' creative processes. Issues of friendship, emotional support, identity, individual and group influence, and psychological satisfaction are all important aspects. Yet while the fabric was not the only thing for these quilters, sources of artistic inspiration were partly linked to sensory stimulation resulting from the medium of cloth and the particular way in which cloth is used in during the quilting process. The role of primary materials in the relationship between artist, medium, sensory experience, and sources of creative inspiration warrants further exploration because it suggests that to create, individuals must first discover a medium that stimulates them and provides a foundation upon which creative processes unfold. Many quilters did not define themselves as artists until they found a particular way to work with a particular medium—fabric—that inspired them. A primary goal for many members of the Pine Needle Quilters was to see it, buy it, play with it, pet it, and manipulate it. The foundation of the event lay in a mosaic of women playing and arranging soft, tangible lines, colors, textures, and patterns brought together in a material they related to, were comfortable with, and genuinely loved. Within this nexus, the fabric was a primary source of inspiration and creativity, which suggests that the relationship and response of the artist to his/her chosen material constitutes a basic dynamic without which creativity cannot emerge and art cannot be produced.

Acknowledgments

I would like to thank Henry Glassie and Sandra Dolby for their helpful feedback, encouragement, and comments on this paper, Michael Owen Jones for emphasizing aesthetic responses, and Virginia Gunn for pointing the way to the concept of the hand. Thanks especially to Billie Hawley, Karen Burton, Catherine Petzak, Leta Polivka, Emily Ede, and Jackie Zbrowski for sharing their time and insights into the quilting process, as well as to the rest of the Pine Needle Quilters whom I could not interview but who graciously allowed me to attend their meetings.

Notes and References

1. John Forrest, "Visual Aesthetics for Five Senses and Four Dimensions: An Ethnographic Approach to Aesthetic Objects," in *Digging into Popular Culture: Theories and Methodologies in Archeology, Anthropology, and Other Fields*, ed. Ray B. Browne and Pat Browne (Bowling Green: Bowling Green State University Popular Press, 1991), 48–57.

2. Sharon Sherman, *Chainsaw Sculptor: The Art of J. Chester "Skip" Armstrong* (Jackson: University Press of Mississippi, 1995); and Linda Pershing, *Sew to Speak: The Fabric Art of Mary Milne* (Jackson: University Press of Mississippi, 1995).

3. See, for example, Kristin M. Langellier, "Appreciating Phenomenology and Feminism: Researching Quiltmaking and Communication," *Human Studies* 17 (1994):65–80.

4. Her work that I refer to specifically is Joyce Ice, "Women's Aesthetics and the Quilting Process," in *Feminist Theory and the Study of Folklore*, ed. Susan Tower Hollis, Linda Pershing, and M. Jane Young (Urbana: University of Illinois Press, 1993), 166–77.

5. This research was conducted over a ten-week period. Meetings were held once a week on Monday nights.

6. Joyce Ice, "Splendid Companionship and Practical Assistance," in *Quilted Together: Women, Quilts, and Communities*, ed. Joyce Ice and Linda Norris (Delhi, NY: Delaware County Historical Association, 1989), 6–24; and Gayle Davis, "Women in the Quilt Culture: An Analysis of Social Boundaries and Role Satisfaction," *Kansas History: A Journal of the Central Plains* 13/1 (1990):5–12.

7. Susan Stewart, "Sociological Aspects of Quilting in Three Brethren Churches in Southeastern Pennsylvania," *Pennsylvania Folklife* 23/3 (1974):15–29; see also Davis, 1990; Ice, 1989.

8. Leta Polivka of McCall, Idaho, interview by author, 26 May 1996, tape recording in author's possession.

9. Jackie Zbrowski of McCall, Idaho, interview by author, 2 June 1996, tape recording in author's possession.

10. Catherine Petzak of McCall, Idaho, interview by author, 27 May 1996, tape recording in author's possession.

11. Pat Ferrero, Elaine Hedges, and Julie Silber, *Hearts and Hands: The Influence of Women and Quilts on American Society* (San Francisco: Quilt Digest Press, 1987).

12. Doris J. Dyen, "The Allison Park Quiltmakers," in *Craft and Community: Traditional Arts in Contemporary Society*, ed. Shalom D. Staub (Harrisburg: The Commission, 1988), 63–70 , esp. 64.

13. Billie Hawley of McCall, Idaho, interview by author, 27 May 1996, tape recording in author's possession.

14. Polivka, 1996.

15. Karen Burton of McCall, Idaho, interview by author, 26 May 1996, tape recording in author's possession.

16. Jane Przybysz, "Quilts and Women's Bodies: Dis-eased and Desiring," in *Bodylore*, ed. Katharine Young (Knoxville: University of Tennessee Press, 1993), 165–84, esp. 168.

17. Petzak, 1996.

18. Yvonne J. Milspaw, "Jennie's Quilts: The Interface of Folk and Popular Tradition in the Work of a New York Quiltmaker," *New York Folklore* 8/1–2 (1982):11–23.

19. Zbrowski, 1996.

20. Emily Ede of McCall, Idaho, interview by author, 2 June 1996, tape recording in author's possession.

21. Hawley, 1996.

22. Petzak, 1996.

23. See, for example, Billie J. Collier and Helen H. Epps, *Textile Testing and Analysis* (Upper Saddle River, NJ: Merrill, an imprint of Prentice-Hall, 1999).

24. Zbrowski, 1996.

25. Burton, 1996.

26. Petzak, 1996.

27. Polivka, 1996.

28. Ede, 1996.

29. Hawley, 1996.

30. For a folkloristic emphasis on collecting as creative behavior, see Stacy Tidmore, "Making One's Way: Souvenir Traditions among Elvis Fans" (M.A. thesis, Indiana University, 1999). For an introduction to a cultural studies/literary perspective, see *The Cultures of Collecting*, ed. John Elsner and Roger Cardinal (Cambridge: Harvard University Press, 1994); and Susan Stewart, *On Longing: Narratives of the Miniature, the Gigantic, the Souvenir, the Collection* (Durham and London: Duke University Press, 1993).

31. See, for example, Werner Muensterberger, *Collecting: An Unruly Passion: Psychological Perspectives* (Princeton: Princeton University Press, 1994) for a psychological perspective. For an emphasis on connoisseurship and collection value, see Shirley Z. Johnson, "A Textile Collector's Approach to Collecting," *Arts of Asia* 25/4 (1995):126–39.

32. Ice, 1989, 23.

33. Przybysz, 179.

34. Polivka, 1996.

35. Burton, 1996.

36. Zbrowski, 1996.

37. Petzak, 1996.

38. Burton, 1996.

39. Polivka, 1996.

40. Zbrowski, 1996.

41. Sandra K. D. Stahl, "A Quiltmaker and Her Art," in *Indiana Folklore: A*

Reader, ed. Linda Dégh (Bloomington: Indiana University Press, 1980), 46–73, esp. 64.

42. Polivka, 1996.
43. Hawley, 1996.
44. Burton, 1996.
45. Zbrowski, 1996.
46. Ede, 1996.
47. Stewart, 1974; Dyen, 1988; Davis, 1990; Langellier, 1992; Przybysz, 1993; Ice, 1993.
48. Petzak, 1996.
49. Davis, 1990.
50. Zbrowski, 1996.
51. Polivka, 1996.
52. Petzak, 1996.
53. Burton, 1996.
54. Ede, 1996.
55. Petzak, 1996.
56. Burton, 1996.
57. Ede, 1996.

✾ ✾ ✾

Quilts and Their Stories: Revealing a Hidden History

Marsha MacDowell

Keynote address given at the Annual Seminar, American Quilt Study Group, East Lansing, Michigan, October 15, 1999

Embedded in every quilt are many, many stories. Quilts contain stories about the quiltmaker; stories about why, when, and how the quilt was made and used; stories about where the fabric and patterns were acquired: the list of stories goes on. Some of these stories—or histories—can be deduced by examining the physical evidence—such as words and pictures—directly presented on the quilts. Some stories, however, are known only through other sources such as household or diary accounts, state quilt inventory records, manufacturing records of the production of fabrics or patterns, and newspapers. In the last twenty years, the use of another source of quilt stories—oral histories—has greatly expanded our knowledge about quilts, their makers, and their production and use. In this lecture I will examine not only ways in which oral accounts are critical to our understanding of quilting but also the challenges oral accounts sometimes pose in building a body of quilt scholarship.

But first, let me share with you a story. It is a personal experience story. This past June, my husband and I, accompanied by our nineteen-year-old daughter Marit, were on a business trip in South Africa. After a long week of meetings with museum colleagues in Cape Town, we took Saturday to drive the tip of the Cape of Good Hope (check your maps or globe—it is the southernmost tip of Africa). The entire tip is now protected as a large nature reserve supporting incredible vegetation and much wildlife. As we paid our admission at the reserve entrance, we noticed large posted signs warning people not to feed the roaming baboons because they are aggressive and could be dangerous. When we got to the parking lot at the very tip of the Cape, we saw quite a few baboons, especially near the food stand and lots of people around were taking pictures of them. Well, as we were exiting the lot and driving slowly by one sitting on top of a car, Marit and I rolled down our windows to take a picture. Before I could even get my camera focused, that baboon, with a single quick bound, came right in my window, hopped over my shoulder to the back seat, plunked down beside Marit, and started ripping into our bag of snacks. Needless to say, Marit managed to quickly unbuckle her seat belt and hopped out of the car as did my husband Kurt and I.

For a few frantic moments we did not know what to do as the baboon sat there, with the car running on idle, ripping into food bags. To make matters worse, since our windows were down and the car doors were open, some more baboons started coming toward the car. Bystanders were yelling conflicting advice (like do not aggravate them, go get the park guards, close/open the windows, close/open the doors, etc.) but fortunately, after throwing my backpack out of the car and carrying some of our food, the baboon hopped out. We jumped in the car, rolled up the windows as quickly as possible, and drove away! We were sort of dazed but laughing; we could not believe how fast it had all happened and that Marit actually had just been sitting in the back seat strapped in next to a baboon! So—how is that for a wildlife adventure? PS: We all decided that they need to revise the park's baboon warning signs with a new added line that says "Keep your car windows rolled up!"

Now, this version of an incident that really happened is essentially the rendition I emailed from South Africa to my family back home. Since we left the park I have retold that story a few times myself, conscious that in each retelling I altered the story slightly—sometimes to add or shorten it (because of the time allotted to telling the story), sometimes to tailor elements to the audience who was listening (who either needed to have more or less explanation about certain parts with which they were either familiar or unfamiliar). For instance, to a resident of Cape Town there was a predictably shared understanding of South African wildlife, the Cape, and perhaps inexperienced or uninformed tourist actions. When I told it to our Michigan State University Museum colleagues (who include mammalogists), the story elicited shared stories about wildlife behavior. Sharing the story with other world or frequent travelers prompted stories about the unusual adventures often encountered during travel.

I also have been present when Kurt and Marit told their versions of the experience. Basically their story was the same but they told it with some slight variations. Their memories and their perceptions differed in small but significant ways: the number of baboons that were approaching the car, the distance of the baboons from the car, the number of bystanders, etc. Yet, by the end of the summer, the oft-told story, despite its many subtle variations, had retained its key elements: the suddenness of a wild animal's actions, the comic quality of Marit being seat-belted next to a baboon, our immediate inability to figure out a solution, our ingenuity in getting out of a fix, and our relief that the episode ended with no one being hurt and nothing being damaged. Within our immediate family, the story is used to illustrate our shared delight in encountering new environments as well as to reinforce the acknowledged personality characteristics of each of us (as in our daughter's distinctive laughter which was enjoyed by the strangers witnessing our dilemma).

Later in the summer, at the annual Labor Day reunion of the MacDowell family, one of my brothers who lives in Washington, D.C. and who had received my original emailed story, told me he got a great laugh out of the story. Moreover, he had told that story to a lot of his friends and co-workers. Now, the story, which had been a personal experience story, was being retold by someone who was not even there! I wondered how he would tell it, what elements were important to him and his sense of his audience, and why did he tell it? Was it to illustrate another point of his own? Was it to convey that he had this crazy older sister who was always traveling off to distant parts of the globe and having adventures not common in a day-to-day existence? I do not know and can not answer, because I was not there to hear his telling of my tale.

So what does this story about baboons at the Cape of Good Hope have to do with quilts and their stories? Actually a lot. Our ability to understand quilt-related stories has everything to do with our understanding of the origins of the stories, the relationship of the story to the teller, the uniqueness of the story, the reasons for telling the story, and, lastly, the audiences who hear the story.

Most of us are engaged in quilt research because we are interested in not only the textiles as works of art and exemplars of fabrics and techniques, but also as the vehicles to uncover stories which help enrich our understanding of our world, both past and present. We seek to learn about the lives of individual quiltmakers, owners, and users, about women's history, about cultural history, about textile history, about the relationship between the fabricated pieces and the spoken and written word—to name but a few quilt-related interests. In those searches, the collection, documentation, and analysis of orally-told stories can help to further that understanding.

Perhaps one of the first, and best-known, publications based on research entailing extensive interviews with quilters was Patricia Cooper and Norma Bradley Buferd's *The Quilters: Women and Domestic Art: An Oral History* published in 1977. Cooper and Buferd interviewed approximately thirty quilters in their homes and community centers scattered across New Mexico and Texas. Some were interviewed for a short time and some over the course of a couple of days. The stories quilters told of their own quilting experiences as well as the experiences of their relatives, friends, and neighbors revealed both intensely personal and individual histories. When taken as a whole, their orally-told histories revealed many experiences that, for this set of women, were common or typical: using cotton gleaned directly from the fields for the filling or batting of quilts; participating in Wednesday night, church-based quilting groups; learning to quilt—often before ten years of age; the use of recycled fabrics and the treasured use of new fabrics; the prevalence of Lone Star or Star of Bethlehem quilts; community traditions such as making Friendship and Album quilts; the closeness of mother and daughters through quilting; making and using quilts as fund-raisers for community needs or to help those in need; making quilts as a means of finding solace in the face of illness, tragedy, death, and hardship; and the necessity of quilts for warmth (especially in the dugout homes many pioneer families lived in). The basic stories had many, many similarities because the women themselves shared many common life experiences. Through these commonly-told stories

Quilts and Their Stories

connected to quilting, we gain a wider glimpse into what life must have been like for these women who were among some of the first families, post-Native settlement, to establish homesteads in this part of the country.

Yet the stories also reveal experiences that were completely unique to some individuals and not shared by the other women. These are the stories that we understand are deeply personal and reveal more about the individual and less about the community. Listen to the following three accounts.

The first story helps us understand the reasons why a quilter prefers to use one pattern over another:

> Before my father died, he was a lumberman; we lived in a forest near Lufkin. He built our house. It was a log house and it was plenty big, two fireplaces. He had plans all laid out to make it bigger when the family grew and when he could get the time.
>
> He put such care in fittin' everything just perfect. He always whistled when he worked. Sometimes he and Mama would whistle harmony. We all turned to listen to that when it happened. I was always allowed to choose if I wanted to work outside with Papa or inside with Mama. When I was younger I dearly loved workin' outside with him. Well, every time I make a Log Cabin I think of him. It just comes naturally, making a Log Cabin.[1]

Likewise, the second story I am going to share also reveals why a particular pattern is preferred, but this story also shows how quilts can serve as reminders of shared experiences and of individuals:

> I like straight-line quilts. The first quilt I ever worked on was like that. Papa was setting up fence around the place he homesteaded, and Mama decided to make this fence-row quilt. That's when I started piecing, when I was five years old. And it was a piece of work we all did together. I asked her in later years what she did with those stitches. She said she just left them in the quilt, 'cause she liked to see them reminding her of that time. She never took out any of our stitches, though maybe she had to quilt a little closer to make it look right.[2]

The third story presents to us the ingenuity of the maker in constructing a design and the meaning that quilt had for her and her sons. It also tells us about the husband's mixed feelings about a man's role in quilting:

> My husband tells about the time he got sick with the measles. He was six years old. His mother set him to piecing a quilt and every other block he set in red polka-dot pattern. Said it was his measles quilt. He wouldn't like me to tell it now I know. But lots of cold nights when I'm at the quiltin' frame on one side of the fire, he pulls his big old chair up on the other side and cuts pieces for me. He's even done a pit of piecin' from time to time.
>
> It's a sight, that big old long-legged man with his boot toes turned in to make a lap to do his piecework on.
>
> We've got a fair long road from the highway and three loud dogs out there. They all always sound off when somebody turns up our road. And let me tell you, he can git rid of that work quicker than a gnat can bat an eye, when them dogs commence to barkin'.
>
> Plumb tickles me.[3]

Of course, these stories put a human face on quilting, reveal the person behind the needle and thread, and give voice to the motivations, inspirations, beliefs, and attitudes of the quilt's maker. Nevertheless, when we enjoy the stories, we recognize them as unique. For instance, we understand that the story about the red and white quilt called the "measles quilt" was about a distinctive work and name; it was not a pattern name or choice of fabric commonly made by other quilters in this community or elsewhere when they or members of their family were afflicted with the same illness. In other words, what we can glean from this story is limited by how that story was collected and the way the story was presented or interpreted. Perhaps Buferd and Cooper actually gathered other stories about the making of "measles quilts" and just did not report them in the book, or perhaps the tradition existed but Buferd and Cooper did not happen to collect other stories, or perhaps it was just simply a unique story. Though it amuses me to think about the possibility of a tradition of making red and white polka-dotted quilts when someone has measles—after all it is plausible since measles is such a common childhood illness and I have heard many other stories related to techniques used to comfort children with measles or chickenpox—at this point in time there is only this one known published story about a single instance.

Over the course of the last twenty years there have been many other studies, published and unpublished, which have been based wholly or partly on diaries, memoirs, and oral histories. My own studies of quiltmaking have heavily relied on such sources. These sources are replete with unique stories of quiltmaking experiences, some of which have been incredibly compelling as potential indicators of perhaps more widely-shared experiences. I encountered one such one, courtesy of a reference from Nancy Hornback, in the course of research on quiltmaking among Native peoples in the United States and Canada. It is as follows. A Choctaw woman, Sarah Ann Harlan, reminisced in 1913 to Muriel Wright about a quilting party she attended in 1857 shortly after she moved to Skullyville, the Choctaw Indian Agency west of Fort Smith, Arkansas. Her memoirs, published in *The Chronicles of Oklahoma*, recalled:

> So, not long after this, there came a lot of Indian women to invite me to a quilting. Quilting was the order of the day then, and they always had a big pow wow. The men furnished the meat and barbecued it, and wild game as well. Well, I went to the first one, and saw barbecued beeves, hogs, venison, and thought it enough to satisfy an army. I was always treated royally. The Indians kept coming until I verily believe there must have been six or seven hundred people at this quilting. They had arbors all over the ground and the quilts were hung in them. They were beautifully pieced. Here I prided myself that my mother had taught me to quilt beautifully; I knew my quilting would not be criticized. An old [Choctaw] lady by the name of [Susan] Hall who ran a hotel at Skullyville, and who, by the way, was my brother's mother-in-law, was one of the examiners of the quilting. When she got to me she said, "Well, you quilt fine." I remarked to her, "mother taught me to quilt."
>
> Now you see, this was bordering on civilization. Prizes were given to the best quilters. I received a strand of white and red beads. They were real pretty. I wish that I had had sense enough to preserve those beads. Even to this day I watch bead counters to see if I can duplicate those beads. I would enjoy myself at these big gatherings, but they failed to drive the tears away. You know old man Time does all those healing properties.[4]

After first encountering this account, I so badly hoped that I would come across photographs of pow wow quilting bees, other written memoirs or orally told stories, or perhaps newspaper accounts of that event and ones like it. I had hoped to find that quilting pow wows were common among Choctaw, or even among Southern nations, or, better yet, throughout Native communities. Alas, though I found quite a bit of data on other types of historical displays of Native quilts in other settings and even information on quilts shown at contemporary pow wows, I have yet to find additional corroborating evidence of historical quilting pow wows. Thus, as a scholar, I could only report that there has been a long-standing tradition of the public display of quilts in many different tribal settings. Sarah Ann Harlan's beautifully-told account of the quilting pow wow is, until proven otherwise, a personal story of a unique event.

Early in this year [1999], one person's story became the basis for the book, *Hidden in Plain View: A Secret Story of Quilts and the Underground Railroad* written by Jacqueline Tobin and Raymond Dobard, Ph.D., that has swept the nation and captured a wide popular audience. Sales were propelled by appearances by the authors in advance of the publication when they would not reveal the "secret" prior to the book's issuance and in post-publication appearances on such shows as *The Oprah Winfrey Show* and in reviews in *USA Today* and *The New York Times*. By early October 1999, the book was listed as #662 of the top-selling books on the amazon.com sales list. Tonight I am not going to re-analyze all of the criticisms this book has already received by those engaged in the scholarly study of textile history. I think, however, it is worth examining the dangers of using one person's story—without any corroborating evidence—as every person's story. Essentially, Tobin and Dobard present Mrs. Ozella McDaniel Williams's story of the "Underground Railroad Code" or "Quilt Code" [the authors' title, it is unclear if it was what Mrs. Williams called it] as, and I am quoting here from the jacket cover to the book, "proof that some slaves were involved in a sophisticated network that melded African textile traditions with American quilt practices and created a potent result: African American quilts with patterns that conveyed messages that were, in fact, essential tools for escape along the Underground Railroad."[5]

Thirty-three pages into their book, long after presenting "the code" essentially as fact, the authors give this brief two-paragraph qualifier that it is in fact just a theory:

> Based on my knowledge as a quilter/historian, Jacki's expertise in women's stories, and our combined research, we were able to formulate a theory of how this Quilt Code may have worked for slaves escaping on the Underground Railroad. Our interpretation of the code is based in part upon in-

Quilts and Their Stories

formed conjecture. While we believe that our research and the piecing together of our findings present a strong viable case, we do not claim that our "deciphering" of the code is infallible. Nor do we insist that our perspective is the only one for viewing the code. We have written the book in a way that encourages questions. We leave room for the reader to add her/his own ideas and thereby contribute to the growing body of knowledge. In the spirit of quiltmaking, we invite you to join us in juxtaposing ideas so that patterns and meanings are revealed.[6]

While the authors claim that "Ideally, we would have several of the special slave-made quilts containing the patterns and stitching mentioned in Ozella's story-code to analyze," they provide a variety of excuses why there are no extant examples.[7] Ignoring the fact that oral histories, diaries, and photographs could have also provided corroborating evidence, the authors admit that "We have thus found ourselves obliged to reverse conventional procedures, having to present a theory before finding a wealth of tangible evidence."[8]

The remaining 175 pages of the book are devoted to providing the reader with information on how some scholars have found ways in which African-Americans have embedded other "secret" information in various elements of culture, including quilts. The authors also present examples of contemporary quilts made by African-Americans, including those by Dobard himself, using the same patterns. The publication is presented as a scholarly work, filled with citations to other work on the Underground Railroad, African textiles, secret symbols, African-American culture in general, and African-American quilts in particular.

What is troubling though is that at no time is Mrs. Williams's story corroborated or is information given about Dobard and Tobin's efforts to do so, particularly within her own family and community. For instance, we learn Williams had siblings but we do not hear if they had even been asked whether they knew the story. Did Williams have any offspring? Had they heard the story? If not, why? Why did Williams entrust Tobin with the story? Did she ever share the story with other quilters? If not, why? Also troubling is that Dobard and Tobin spend four pages examining how "The Code" parallels the quilted work of the fictitious Clara of the children's story *Sweet Clara and the Freedom Quilt*.[9] Presenting the popular children's book as a valuable source of data to support the code is to make a mockery of quilt scholarship and of the value of oral histories in that scholarship.

In a foreword to *Hidden in Plain View*, Floyd Coleman writes that "Tobin and Dobard have taken quilt scholarship to another level."[10] Tobin and Dobard will have shared "the code" with thousands but, despite Coleman's assertion, they will not have advanced quilt scholarship. Quite the opposite, they will have embedded in our collective public mind a story so romantic and compelling that it, like the story of Paul Bunyan, will move into the realm of stories that, despite their origin, become part of our belief system. Obviously, unless the wide-scale distribution of *Hidden in Plain View* flushes out other corroborating evidence of the "Quilt Code,"—which it has yet to do—Mrs. Williams's story, like that of the Choctaw quilter Sarah Harlan, should remain just a wonderfully told personal story.

The ramifications, however, of the national promotion of this story as fact, not theory, and the dangers of accepting Mrs. Williams's story as every person's story has already been seen in numerous forms this year. Let me just share how embedded this story has become in our nation's conscience.

On February 22 of this year [1999], an article, entitled "Black History Gets Creative," in the *Lansing State Journal* reported on a Black History Month Project at a local elementary school:

> Students learned slaves used specific quilt patterns to relay messages to escaping slaves. A quilt with a bow tie or hourglass for instance was a sign to runaway slaves that the area's residents were friendly and could be trusted. . . . "Each quilt told a message" said the teacher who developed the lesson, "And it was a message they were to memorize on their escape to freedom.". . . Students used donated fabric to trace and copy the nine patterns slaves used to navigate the Underground Railroad, an escape network carved out by abolitionists.[11]

About a month later I received a call from a member of the education staff at a regional public museum in Michigan. The individual wanted to know what else could go along with the Quilt Code blocks they were putting in the Underground Railroad resource kit they were preparing for loan to schools.[12] The readers' comment section of amazon.com included this August 15, 1999 testimonial from a woman in California:

The information was an eye opener and just confirmed what we already knew. We are a strong, beautiful, intelligent people descended from survivors of slavery. Imagine using codes and patterns to lead a people through the Underground Railroad and unto Canada and freedom. My sister and I are taking up quilting to keep the tradition alive.[13]

Then, just this past weekend, while at a national arts conference in Boston, I heard from the head of a major community-based youth arts program in Pittsburgh that the kids had worked all summer on quilts just like those which had been used on the Underground Railroad.[14]

Certainly, as we turn to oral histories as sources of data about quilting history, we must remember to consider a number of important factors when we begin to present and analyze that data. Who originally tells the story, when, where, why; are there other stories that are similar and, if so, what are the variations and similarities; and who retells the story, why, and in what context. All must be considered. A quilt-related oral history, like any other source material, is but one piece of data in the testing of a theory or in the description or analysis of a quilt topic. It must be supported by solid scholarship that corroborates and substantiates the story.

Now, to bring us all back to my story of the close encounter with the baboon in South Africa. Does every visitor to the Cape of Good Hope, who does not know better, end up with a baboon in the back seat of their car? Well, I hope that neither have I suggested that scenario nor have you construed that. I do hope, however, that if you ever visit that parking lot at the southern most tip of Africa, you will remember to keep your windows rolled up. Thank you.

Notes

1. Patricia Cooper and Norma Bradley Buferd, *The Quilters, Women and Domestic Art: An Oral History* (Garden City, NY: Doubleday 1977; paperback edition, Anchor Press/Doubleday, 1978), 65.

2. Ibid., 39–42.

3. Ibid., 39.

4. Muriel H. Wright "Sarah Ann Harlan: From Her Memoirs of Life in the Indian Territory," *The Chronicles of Oklahoma* 39, no. 2 (1956), 304–05. [Thanks to Nancy Hornback for bringing this to my attention.]

5. Jacqueline Tobin and Raymond Dobard, Ph.D., *Hidden in Plain View: A Secret*

Story of Quilts and the Underground Railroad (New York: Doubleday, 1999), jacket cover.

6. Ibid., 33.

7. Ibid.

8. Ibid.

9. Deborah Hopkinson, *Sweet Clara and the Freedom Quilt* (New York: Alfred A. Knopf, 1993).

10. Floyd Coleman, "The Importance of the Decorative Arts in African American History," in *Hidden in Plain View*, 5.

11. *Lansing State Journal*, 22 February 1999, 4B.

12. Personal communication with staff member of Kalamazoo (Michigan) Valley Museum, March 1999.

13. Reader's comment on Amazon.com, 15 August 1999.

14. Personal communication with Joshua Green, 8 October 1999.

Authors and Editor

Ethel Ewert Abrahams holds a B.A. in printmaking and a M.A. in art education. She has taught art at the college level and authored publications including *Frakturmalen und Schönschreiben,* a book on Mennonite Fraktur art and penmanship. Ethel is also a quiltmaker and quilt lecturer and curated the traveling exhibit *Better Choose Me: Collecting and Creating with Tobacco Fabric Novelties, 1880-1920.* PO Box 178, North Newton, KS 67117.

Xenia E. Cord has degrees in history and English and in folklore and American studies. She is a lecturer in folklore at Indiana University. She owns Legacy Quilts, an antique quilts brokerage, and partners with Annette Baker to produce Quilt America, an annual event in Indianapolis since 1990. Xenia considers herself a "closet quiltmaker," while her efforts as quilt historian/research/writer have appeared regularly in quilt publications. 2217 Avalon Ct., Kokomo, IN 46902-3101.

Lisa Gabbert, a doctoral candidate in Folklore and American Studies at Indiana University, is interested in the dynamic of tradition and creativity in everyday life, particularly as manifested in folk art/material culture and narrative. Her dissertation research focuses on the ways in which people use objects and narratives to create different senses of community in the public sphere. 1000 West 7th Street, Bloomington, IN 47404.

Virginia Gunn, the editor of *Uncoverings,* has a M.S. in clothing and textiles and a Ph.D. in history. She is a professor and the director of graduate studies for the School of Family and Consumer Sciences at the University of Akron in Ohio. Her research focuses on women's history and on nineteenth-century American textiles, costume, and decorative arts. 215 Schrank Hall, University of Akron, Akron, OH 44325-6103.

Phyllis S. Herda, a senior lecturer in women's studies at the University of Auckland, has lived in New Zealand since 1981. Her academic work in anthropology and history centers around gender, power, and colonialism, and she holds degrees from colleges in Arizona, New Zealand, and Australia. Phyllis is currently studying women's quilting in Polynesia under a Marsden Fund grant from the Royal Society of New Zealand. University of Auckland, Private Bag 92019, Auckland, New Zealand.

Laurel Horton has a M.S. in library science and a M.A. in folklore. Self-employed as a researcher and consultant, Laurel presents grants workshops to nonprofit groups and educators for the Polaris Corporation. She has served AQSG as both president and editor of *Uncoverings*. A frequent author and lecturer, her research focuses on regional variations in quiltmaking traditions. 302 East South Third Street, Seneca, SC 29678-3515.

Marsha MacDowell, Ph.D., a professor of art, is curator of folk arts at the Michigan State University Museum. Marsha coordinates the Michigan Quilt Project and the Michigan Traditional Arts Program. She has served AQSG as president, vice-president, and board member. Her research focuses on traditional arts of Native Americans, the Great Lakes region, and South Africa. Michigan State University Museum, Michigan State University, East Lansing, MI 48824-1045.

Susan Price Miller, a quiltmaker and designer, owns the Dusty Miller Designs pattern business. An active member of the Pella Area Quilters Guild and the Iowa Quilters Guild, Susan is currently helping to preserve the quilt collection at the Scholte House Museum. A teacher, lecturer, and writer with a B.A. and advanced work in history, she specializes in research on Iowa quilts and quilters. 1006 Monroe Street, Pella, IA, 50219-1147.

Rachel K. Pannabecker is director of Kauffman Museum and assistant professor of social science at Bethel College in Kansas. She earned her Ph.D. in textiles and clothing and her research on Native American ribbonwork and on fashion theories appears in the *Clothing and Textiles Research Journal*. Rachel quilts with The Quilters of First Mennonite Church, McPherson, Kansas. Kauffman Museum, Bethel College, North Newton, KS 67117.

Index

Page numbers in **boldface** refer to illustrations.

Alexander, Mrs. J. F. (Emma Scott), 8, 11, 14; her family, 9-10
Ayres, Kathern (Lucretia King), 111-14

Baseball Heroes: Ty Cobb, Walter Johnson, and John P. Wagner, 94
Bedient, Jennie, 141
Benberry, Cuesta, 108
Beverly, William, 32
Bridenbaugh, Carl, 31
Bronner, Simon, 99
Buferd, Norma Bradley, 158, 160
Button, Ida McDivitt, 94
Button, May, 92, **93**
Byrd, Mrs. J. W. (Personne "Sonny" Magee), 8, 11-16, 22; her family, 10

Carpenter, Lillie Belle Shaffer, 126
Carver, Miss Nora, 8, 22
Cary, Mrs. F. M. (Annie Mildred Fant), 8, 11-12, 14-15, 22; her family, 9
The Chronicles of Oklahoma, 161
Cigarette Brands:
  Camel, 98
  Egyptienne Luxury, 89
  Hassan, 96, 98-99
  Mecca, 99
  Nebo, 89, 99
  Old Mill, 89
  Omar, 96, **97**, 99
  Turkey Red, 89
  Zira, **87**, 88-89, 99

Cigarette Companies:
  American Tobacco Company, 87-88, 92, 96, 98
  Liggett & Myers, 88
  P. Lorillard, 88-89
  R. J. Reynolds, 88, 98
  W. Duke, Sons & Co., 86
Clark, George Rogers, 47
Coleman, Floyd, 164
Colonial Craftsman, The, 31
Colonial Quilts, 108, 116, **117**, 118, 120-21, 125
Colonial Quilts and Decorative Needle Work, 115-16, 125-26
Companies, quilt-related:
  Aunt Martha, 120
  The Colonial Pattern Company, 120
  Colonial Readicut Quilt Block Company, 120
  Home Art Company, 125-26
  Home Art Studios, 107-32, esp. 125-30
  Ladies Art Company, 113, 115-16, 118
  Needleart Company, 124-25
  Practical Patchwork, 132
  Rainbow Quilt Block Company, 113
Comforter, 92, **94**
Cooper, Patricia, 158, 160
Coverlids or rugs, 43
Cozart, Dorothy, 80
Crisp, Miss Annie, 20-21

171

Dawkins, John, 39, **41**
Des Moines Register and Tribune Syndicate, 124
Dickson, John, 40, **42**
Dobard, Raymond, 162-64
Doyle, Ella Dendy, 18
Doyle, Mrs. James, 18
Dundes, Alan, 149
Dyen, Doris, 140

Editor and Publisher, 124
Exhibits:
    1876 Centennial Exhibition, 81
    1934 Century Of Progress Exposition, 127
    1933 Chicago World's Fair, 126

Fabric, hand, 142-43
Fabric, sensory aspects, 137-38, 141-45
Fabrics:
    broadcloth, **90**
    "Chardonez" rayon, 116
    coarse cloth, 43
    coating, 43
    flannel, 43
    lame, 66
    leather, 29
    linen, 28-31, 34, 43
    linsey-woolsey, 29
    metallic, 66
    sateen, **90**, 115
    satin, 80
    silk jacquard, 80,
    tow, 29
    velvet, 66, 80
    woolen, 31, 43
Favorite Recipes of Quilters, 141
Ferrero, Pat, 140
Forrest, John, 137

Good Housekeeping 1977 Great Quilt Contest, 127
Gottsegen, Jack J., 88
Grier, Katherine C., 5
Gunn, Virginia, 80, 86

Harlan, Sarah Ann, 161-62, 164
Hedges, Elaine, 140
Hidden in Plain View: A Secret Story of Quilts and the Underground Railroad, 162-63
Hill, George Washington, 98
Hite, Joist, 32
Holleman, Frances, 8, **9**, 13-14
Hollingsworth, Ann, 32
Hope Winslow's Quilt Book, 107-08, **117**, 120, 130, **131**
Hopkins, Miss Maude, 15
Hornback, Nancy, 161
Household Manufactures in the United States, 1640-1860, 31
Hunt, Miss Clara, 16, 22
Hunter, Mrs. W. S. (Nina Dickinson Lewis), 8, 11-16, 22; her family, 9

Ice, Joyce, 144
Ideal Button & Pleating Company, 109, 113
Iowa Button and Pleating Company, 109, 115, 121, 126, 128, 131-32

Kaeppler, Adrienne, 73

Laird, Pamela, 81
LeCron, Helen Cowles, 121
Linen production, 28-29
Linsey, David, 46
Lupton, Jonathan, 34

Magazines:
    Advertising Age, 128
    American Woman, 85
    Cultivator & Country Gentleman, 83
    Farmers Market Bulletin, 128
    The Farmer's Wife, 128
    Godey's Lady's Book, 83
    Good Housekeeping, 127
    Happy Hours, 85
    Hearth and Home, 85, 89
    The Housekeeper, 83-84
    Jay Bees Magazine, 128, 130

Index

Magazines, *continued*
  Ladies' Home Journal, 84
  Little 'N Big, 128
  Needlecraft, 122, 128
  People's Popular Monthly, 111-13
  The Royal Neighbor, 120
  Rural Progress, 128
  Successful Farming, 120, 128
  Sunshine for Youth, 85
  Wallaces' Farmer, 128
Makey, William, 47
Marseilles spread, 6, 17
McCarey, Mrs. J. F. (Clara Verner), 8, 11-15, 22; her family, 10
McClure, David, 40
McCormick, William: apprenticeship, 32; gambling, 34, 38; his brothers James, John, George, and Andrew, 38, 40, **41**, **42**; his cousin Oliver, 38, 47; Uncle James McCormick, 32, 34; cousin John McCormick, **48**; parents Dr. John and Ann McFarren McCormick, 32; his "pockit book," 32-34, **33**, **36**, **41-42**, 45, **48**; his sporting activities, 35; his father-in-law William Crawford, 35, 44-45, 47; brother-in-law William Harrison, 44-45, 47; sister-in-law Ann Connell, 45; his wife Effelica "Effie" Crawford, 39, **48**; his children, 47, **48**; his home, 39; marriage, 40; trading or teamstering, 35, 38, 43; weaving, 34, 37, 45-46
Milspaw, Yvonne, 141
Murder at the Quilt Show, 141

The Needle Art Vogue Style Book D, 125
Newspapers:
  The Briardale Store News, 114-16, 130
  Capper's Weekly, 119-20
  The Des Moines Register, 121
  Farm and Factory, 16
  Keowee Courier [South Carolina], 1-2, **3**, 4-22

  Lansing State Journal, 164
  The New York Times, 162
  USA Today, 162
  Washington Post, 96, **97**

Old Fashioned Quilts, 115
O'Neill, Rose, 92
The Oprah Winfrey Show, 162
Oral history, 155-65

Patton, James, 32
Pershing, Linda, 138
Pine Needle Quilters, McCall, Idaho, 138-50
  Karen Burton, 140-46, 148-49
  Emily Ede, 142-43, 146, 149
  Billie Hawley, 140, 142-44, 146, 149
  Joyce McFadden, 139
  Catherine Petzak, 140-43, 145, 147-49
  Leta Polivka, 140, 143-47
  Jackie Zbrowski, 140-47
Przybysz, Jane, 141

Quilt patterns, named:
  Bear's Paw, 64
  Blazing Star, 63
  Blossom Time, 118
  Butterfly, 119
  Double T, 113
  Double Wedding Ring, 123
  Drunkard's Path, 64
  Eight-Pointed Star, 63
  Fan, 85
  Grandmother's Fan, 64, **65**
  Grandmother's Flower Garden, 64
  Log Cabin, 159
  Lone Star, 63, **64**, **67**, 115, 117-18, 121, 131, 158
  Mariner's Compass, 64
  Martha Washington's Rose Garden, 119
  May Day Flower Baskets, 118
  Monkey Wrench, 64
  Morning Star, 63, **64**, **67**

Quilt patterns, *continued*
    Pansy Time, 119
    Pieced Star, 63
    Rising Sun, 118, 125
    Slashed Star, 118
    Star, 63, **64**
    Star of Bethlehem, 121, 158
    Star of France, 118, 127
    Starburst, 127
    A Trip to Egypt, 128
    Tulip, 118, **119**
    Virginia Star, 63
    Weathervane, 64
    Yankee Pride, 114
    See also Ver Mehren, repeating unit designs
The Quilters: Women and Domestic Art: An Oral History, 158
Quilting process, 145-47
Quilting groups:
    Chalk Mound, Kansas, quilting group, 94
    Pine Needle Quilters, McCall, Idaho, 138-50
Quilting party, 8
Quilts: album quilts, 158; cigarette silkie quilts, 86-92, **90**, **91**; cot quilts, 73; charity quilts, 4; cigar-ribbon quilts, 80-86, **82**, **84**; crazy quilts, 80-82, 86, 89; friendship quilts, 158; grave quilts, 62-70; Hawaiian-style applique, 64, **66**, 72; log cabin quilts, 83-84, 86; Native-American quilts, 161-62; presentation quilts, 70-73; puff quilts, **65**, 71; tobacco flannel quilts, 92-96, **93**, **94**, **95**
Quilts, of Tonga: as grave decoration and funerary gifts, 62-70; as *tapu* or sacred quilts, 62-70, **63**, **64**, **65**, **66**, **67**, **68**, **69**; as two-layered coverlets, 67, 75; as textile wealth, 70-71, 74; as junior wealth, 73-74; ritual presentation of, 70-73, **71**; Hawaiian-style applique, 64, **66**, 72; cot quilts, 73; puff quilts, **65**, 71-72

Quilts, named:
    Baseball Hero quilt, **95**
    Bible History quilt, 128
    Flag quilt, **90**
    George Washington Mount Vernon quilt, 116
    Indian Motif quilt, **93**
    Measles quilt, 160
    Seals and Crests parlor throw, **91**

Revolutionary War uniforms, 44
Ross, Betsy, 118
Round Robins, 108

Schneider, Jane, 61, 68
Scotch-Irish, 31-32
Sears Quilt Contest, 126, 131
Seneca Institute for Negroes, 11
Seneca Women's Clubs:
    Blossom Girls, 13-17, 19, 22
    Every Tuesday Social Circle, 22
    Gossipers, 13
    Ladies' Aid Society of Presbyterian church, 13-14, 22
    Ladies' Missionary Society of Baptist church, 22
    Once-A-Week Club, 12-13, 22
Sexton, Carlie, 111, 114-15, 118, 130-31
Sherman Antitrust Act of 1890, 87
Sherman, Sharon, 138
Silber, Julie, 140
Smith, Wilene, 85
South Carolina Federation of Women's Clubs, 12
Stahl, Sandra K. D., 145-46
Stewart, Susan, 140
Stribling, Mrs. T. E. (Martha "Mattie" Verner), 8, 11-15, 17, 20-22; her family, 10
Stribling, Mrs. T. S. (Maude Verner), 8, 11; her family, 10
Style Book of Iowa Button & Plaiting Co., Inc., 109-11
Sweet Clara and the Freedom Quilt, 163

Index

Tennant, Richard, 88, 98
Thompson, Mrs. J. H. (Lida Alexander), 1, 6, 11, 15-22; her family, 8
Tilley, Nannie M., 81
Tobin, Jacqueline, 162-64
Tonga: islands, 58, **59**; concept of wealth, 57-58; royal dynasty, 59, 71-73; contact with West, 60, 75; Mormon mission, 61; Peace Corps influence, 61; ceremonies, 70-73
Tonga, traditional textiles: barkcloth, 57, 62, **65**, 68, 72, 74-75 pandanus leaf mats, 57, 68, 72, 74-75
 skirts of flowers, 62
Towle, Marie, 128
Triangular trade, 30
Tryon, Rolla, 31

Underground Railroad, 162-65

Veblen, Thorstein, 79
Ver Mehren, Hubert: background and family, 109-11; photo, **129**; photo with wife, **110**; wife Mary Ellen Jacobs, 109, 125-26, **127**; sister-in-law Lutie, 130, **131**; work with *People's Popular Monthly*, 111-14; work with *The Briardale Store News*, 114-16; his catalogs, 116-21, **117**; death, 130
Ver Mehren marketing names:
 Bettina, 108, 121
 Carol Dean, 108, 115-16
 Mary Jacobs, 108, 125-27, **127**
 Lucretia King, 108, 111-14
 Nancy Lee, 108, 125, 130
 Gertrude May, 108, 120-21
 Marie Towle, 128
 Hope Winslow, 107-08, 130, **131**
Ver Mehren medallion format designs:
 Carol's Delight, 130
 The Eastern Star, 121
 Giant Dahlia, 121, **122**, 129
 Glorious Chrysanthemum, 121
 Glorious Rising Sun, 130
 Royal Aster, 121
 Russian Sunflower, 121
 Sirius Star, 121
Ver Mehren repeating unit designs:
 Clematis, 123
 Cosmos, 123
 Diamond Field Star, 123
 Easter Lily, 123
 Glimmering Christmas Star, 123
 Golden Wedding Ring, 123, **124**
 Interlacing Squares, **123**
 Milky Way Star, 123
 Morning Glory, 123
 Painted Daisy, 123
 Poinsetta [sic], 123
 Rose Star, 123
 Star Bouquet, 123
Ver Mehren quilt design sets:
 "Aunt Dinah's Quilting Album," 116
 "Briardale Designs," 115
 "Master Quilting Album," 120
 "Mother's Old Fashioned Flower Garden," **112**, 113
 "Patchwork Patterns," 113-14
 "Quilting Album," 120

Washington, George, 32, 35
Weaver, Louise Bennett, 121
Webster, Marie, 108, 132
Weiner, Annette B., 61-62, 68, 75
Whatman, John, 34
Williams, Mrs. Ozella McDaniel, 162-64
Willis, James, 39, **41**
Women's Civic Improvement Association, 21
Wright, Catherine and William, 94, **95**

Younker Brothers Department Store, 111, 115

In Appreciation of

Bill Charles Garoutte

*Mill Valley, California
(1922–2000)*

*His patience, support, and good humor
in the years following the death of
AQSG founder Sally Garoutte
strengthened the organization
his wife was so
proud of.*

*Presented by the
Board Members of the
American Quilt Study Group*

Barbara E. Brown
Sara Dillow
Bobbi Finley
Joyce Fisher
Jennifer Goldsborough
Bettina Havig
Bunnie Jordan
Marsha L. MacDowell
Eleanor Malone
Marian Ann J. Montgomery
Pamela M. Pampe
Linda Pumphrey

Fred Calland
1924–1999

Quiltmaker Fred Calland pieced his first top in 1937, growing up in Columbus, Ohio with 13 siblings, but his passion for classical music led to a long career in radio and a position as Senior Producer at National Public Radio in Washington, DC.

In the early 1970s, as interest in quilts and quiltmaking increased, Fred Calland eagerly picked up a needle and turned again to making quilts—quilt tops, to be more precise. Using the repeated block format, he worked with original designs and color combinations. His flair for creating beautiful quilt tops from ugly or misprinted fabric added a wonderful dimension to the late 20th century quilt revival.

Often working in a series, inspiration for his quilt names came from his many interests: opera, gardening, poetry, his family and Cape Cod. With the completion of each top, Fred proudly named it and declared: "not another like it on the block." To his friends and colleagues, that claim is just as appropriate to the quiltmaker himself!

Presented in memory of

Fred Calland

by Karen B. Alexander, Cuesta Benberry, Anne Calland, Hazel Carter, Eileen M. F. Doughty, Susan E. Hinzman, Bunnie Jordon, Katherine M. Seaton, Bethesda Quilters, and The Quilters Hall of Fame

P&B TEXTILES

100% COTTON FABRICS
New Collections

Found only in independent quilt shops
www.pbtex.com

- color Profusion
- color spectrum 2000
- Fiesta
- Jasmine
- Haiku
- COCHECO PRINT WORKS COLLECTION 1881-1885
- Sunday in the Park
- NEW BASICS 2000
- Pine Garland
- Turkish Treasures

Fairfield Processing Corporation, manufacturer of quilting products that endure the test of time.

Future generations will one day look back and affirm that the quality Poly-fil® battings added lasting life to the quilts they cherish today.

Fairfield

PO Box 1130, Danbury, CT 06813
www.poly-fil.com

Schoolhouse Enterprises
Proud Supporters of AQSG & Exclusive Manufacturers of

GRIDDED GEESE© *
...and Other Fun Stuff

for Quilters and Friends of Quilters!
Inspector Cluesew's Mystery Quilts
Reproduction Feed Sacks • Patterns • Books
Monthly $pecial$, too!

http://planetpatchwork.com/store
Call or e-mail us for a Free Sample of Gridded Geese!
Toll-Free: (888) 84GEESE
(609) 628-2256 • FAX: (609) 628-3048
e-mail: Inspectr@cluesew.com

*...a fast, accurate way to mass-produce Flying Geese units up to 24 at once. (No kidding!)

The Front Parlor

Not the newest shop in town but the <u>funnnnest</u>!
*Home to the infamous **Miss Prissy**.*

100% Fine Cotton Fabric
Hoffman, Moda, Timeless Treasures, P & B, RJR
Gift Certificates & Gift Registry Available
Notions, Supplies, Patterns & Books

M-F.....10 a.m. - 6 p.m.   Wed.....10 a.m. - 7 p.m.
Sat.....10 a.m. - 5 p.m.   2nd Sun.....Noon - 4 p.m.

Toll Free: 1-877-313-3773
402-466-9494   E-mail: thefrontparlor@aol.com

The Mercantile Shopping Center
5800 Cornhusker Hwy • Suite 4 • Lincoln NE 68507

✺ ✺ ✺

Uncoverings 2000 *was designed by Dariel Mayer, Knoxville, Tennessee. The text is set in Palatino, a typeface designed for the Stempel foundry in 1950 by Hermann Zapf. The display type is Minion bold condensed, designed for Adobe by Robert Slimbach in 1990. Both fonts were inspired by classical Renaissance typefaces. The book was printed by Thomson-Shore, Inc., Dexter, Michigan on 60-lb Glatfelter Supple Opaque Recycled Natural.*

American Quilt Study Group

- sponsors an exciting seminar each year
- publishes an annual journal, *Uncoverings*
- supports a library and research facility
- produces a series of *Technical Guides*
- publishes the newsletter, *Blanket Statements*
- offers research grants and scholarships
- fosters networking among members

The American Quilt Study Group is a nonprofit organization devoted to uncovering and disseminating the history of quiltmaking as a significant part of American art and culture. AQSG encourages and supports research on quilts, quiltmaking, quiltmakers, and the textiles and materials of quilts.

The American Quilt Study Group is dedicated to preserving the story of quiltmaking—past, present, and future. We invite you to join our ranks!

Levels of Support: $35 Friend; $25 Senior (65+); $25 Student (full time); $100 Associate; $250 Benefactor; $500 Sponsor; $1000 Patron; $2500 Pacesetter; $100 Guild; $250 Guild Benefactor; $1000 Corporate Sponsor; $5000 Corporate Patron; $10,000 Corporate Pacesetter
Canadians add $1.50; all other countries $15.

American Quilt Study Group
35th & Holdrege Street, East Campus Loop
P.O. Box 4737
Lincoln, NE 68504-0737

Phone: 402-472-5361   Fax: 402-472-5428
AQSG2@unl.edu   http://www2.h-net.msu.edu/~aqsg

online library access: http://iris.unl.edu
select: UNL Libraries Catalog